Britain and the Celtic Iron Age

An aerial photograph of Yarnbury hillfort,
Wiltshire, under snow cover and low sun,
revealing very clearly the form of the
ramparts. The outline of a smaller, earlier
fortification circuit, demolished when the
existing fort was built, can be made out in
the interior.

Britain and the Celtic Iron Age

Simon James and Valery Rigby

Published for the Trustees of the British Museum by

BRITISH MUSEUM PRESS

First published in 1997 by British Museum Press
A division of The British Museum Company Ltd
46 Bloomsbury Street, London WC1 3QQ

A catalogue record for this book is available from
the British Library

ISBN 0 7141 2306 4

Designed and typeset by Jeffery Design
Printed in Singapore by Imago Publishing

Front cover One of a pair of cast bronze
handle mounts from the Aylesford bucket. The
bucket, containing cremated bone and three
brooches, was found during the 1880s as a
result of quarrying at Aylesford, Kent. It is
modelled in the round, and the stylisation of
the features has become synonymous with
'Celtic Heads'. H. 60 mm.
Back cover The great hillfort of Maiden Castle,
Dorset.

CONTENTS

PREFACE

The present volume is published on the occasion of the opening of the British Museum's new Celtic Europe gallery (Room 50), created in 1997 to display one of the world's finest collections of European Iron Age 'material culture'.

The gallery contains primarily British antiquities – albeit mostly from the South, with relatively little from Wales or Scotland – with a strong component of material from the territory of the Gauls, who lived in what is today France and neighbouring areas. It also includes related material from Spain and other parts of Iron Age Europe. The period covered is roughly the last six hundred years BC and, for areas like Scotland and Ireland which remained outside the Roman Empire, the first few centuries AD.

The book serves as a companion to many of the displays, and additionally includes aspects such as settlement, daily life and social structure not covered in detail in the gallery. Iron Age art is dealt with in detail in a separate title by Ian Stead, *Celtic Art* (BMP 1985, revised edn 1996).

Such a short work cannot hope to be comprehensive, and the selection of material and approach inevitably reflects our own specialist interests. However, we hope that what follows will serve as an appetiser for further exploration of a fascinating and highly active field of study.

S.T.J. and V.R.,
Bloomsbury, August 1996

Introduction

This book aims to be a brief introduction to the Iron Age of Britain in its wider European context. For these centuries without written record, detailed study of archaeological remains can go a long way to fill gaps in our knowledge but, as will be seen, there is still much to learn, and much that is proving hard to discover.

It also attempts to show how archaeology has, over the last 250 years, contributed to the construction of ideas about the nature of societies in Britain before the Roman invasion, and how new discoveries, reappraisals of old ones, and more sophisticated archaeological ideas are changing our views of the period.

One of the key questions underlying the study of this period is: can Iron Age Britain be called 'Celtic' in any meaningful sense? The idea of a Celtic past in Britain before, and indeed after, the Roman period is an established part of British popular history, and continues to be presented to children in England, as well as in Wales and Scotland. Yet currently many scholars are challenging this idea as misleading, if not actively wrong. Here an attempt is made to review the development of the concept of the 'Celticness' of ancient Britain, and its relevance today.

1 The making of the Celtic Iron Age

1 Victorian statue group of 'Boadicea' and her daughters, presumably charging down the Roman invaders in vengeance. It stands on the Embankment close to the Houses of Parliament in London. The scythes on the wheels are not drawn from any Classical description. They have become part of the popular myth of the Queen of the *Iceni*, who became a powerful national symbol in Britain, which for much of the nineteenth century was ruled over by another queen, who ended her reign as empress of India.

BRITAIN AND THE 'CELTIC' WORLD

Britain on the eve of the Roman conquest, at the close of prehistory, is commonly imagined through a series of vivid images. Druids perform fearsome sacrifices; blue-painted warriors bedecked with gold torcs charge across the landscape in chariots; and perhaps above all, Queen Boudica (Boudicca, 'Boadicea') of the *Iceni*, leads her army into battle against the Roman invaders (fig. 1). These images are at once strange and distant from modern Britain but, to the British, they also seem familiar and close, because they have grown up with them.

Paradoxically, the pre-Roman past of Britain is pleasingly mysterious but at the same time, it seems, generally understood; there is a widely held consensus that it was a Celtic past. Iron Age Britons are seen as part of a vast Celtic commonwealth which then stretched across Europe, a world of peoples who spoke related languages, and who shared a distinctive set of values, social institutions, spirituality, art and other aspects of life and culture (fig. 2). Ancient Celts may generally have been non-literate, but they were eloquent, creative and artistic, fearless free spirits at one with nature, the romantic antithesis of our own literate, urban, industrial civilisation.

This Celtic Iron Age Britain is also widely felt to be at one with both earlier and later times, stretching back into the mists of the Bronze Age, through the supposed association of Druids with Stonehenge, and forward to the worlds of Arthur and early Wales. It has affinities to the ancient Irish myths, the culture of the wild Highlanders of Scotland, and through all these to the modern 'Celtic West'.

In a sense, then, Iron Age Britain and Ireland seem to form an essential pivot, the centre of Celtdom in time and space – although not necessarily the heart or the apogee of Celtic cultural achievement. The British Isles in antiquity form the common ground, the linkage between, on the one hand, the wider, largely continental Celtic world, which is almost entirely a feature of the Iron Age; and on the other hand, the medieval and modern 'Celtic' world, which is almost entirely confined to the British Isles.

These widely familiar images, ideas and connections are not simply truths that have come down to us directly from the remote past. No substantial writings of the Britons survive – we believe they were largely non-literate. The physical remains of the artefacts, settle-

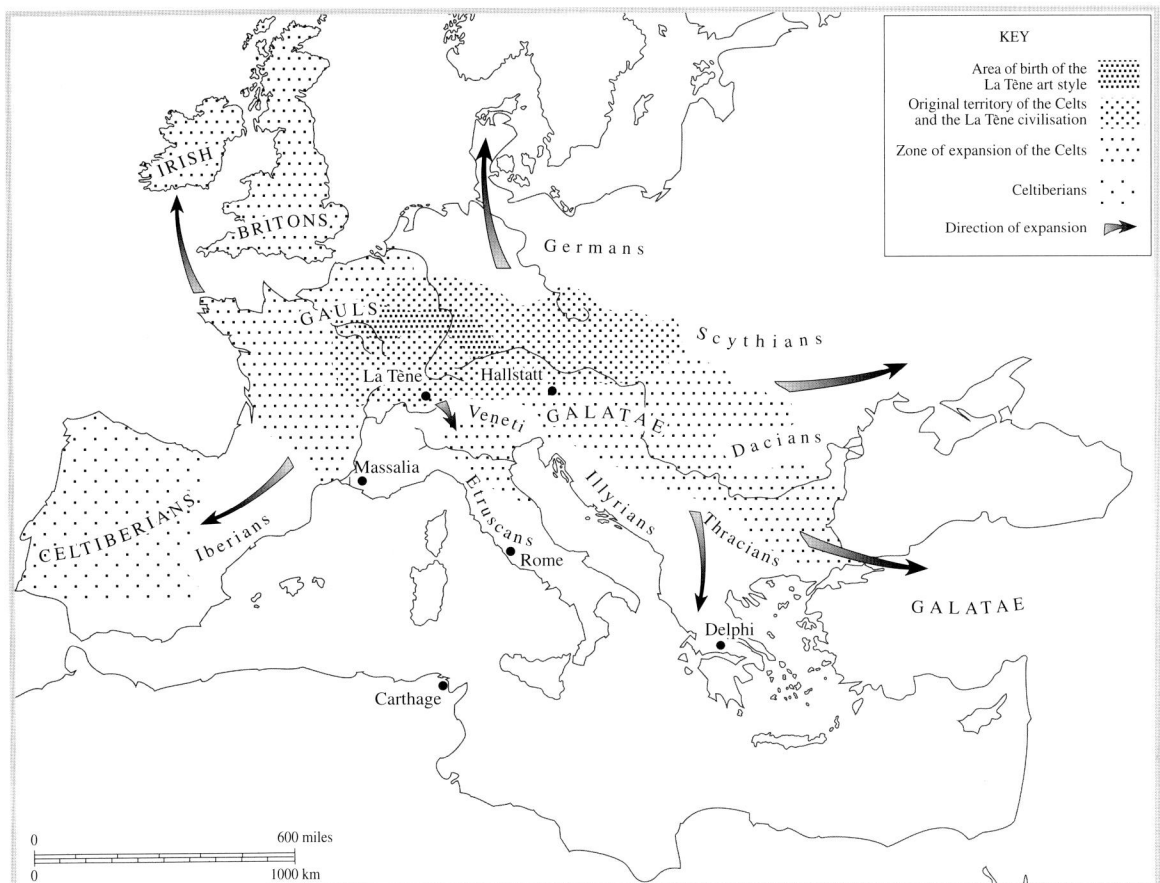

2 The 'Celtic world' of the Iron Age as it has been widely envisaged in recent decades, assuming migration of Celtic peoples in almost all directions from a central 'homeland'. This is now seen by most British archaeologists as, at best, an oversimplification. (Based on Megaw and Megaw 1989, fig. 2)

ments and landscapes they created have only been sought, identified and interpreted since the stereotypes were established. So, how do we come to have such impressions?

WRITING HISTORY

We do not discover history. We identify evidence, and then *create* history, using the fragments of surviving information, and our understanding of the contemporary world and human societies, to make narratives and explanations of what we *think* happened. Consequently, histories inevitably reflect the preoccupations, preconceptions and blind-spots of the people and the times which produce them.

The notion that peoples in the British Isles, both ancient and modern, can be described as 'Celtic' is a surprisingly recent reconstruction, or even invention; no-one but a few isolated scholars referred to the Irish or British as 'Celtic' until about 1700. Before that date 'Celtic' had normally been applied only to ancient peoples dwelling on the Continent. Where, then, does the idea of Celtic Britons come from? What is the role of recent people, scholars and others, in creating a

3 Julius Caesar (100–44 BC) on a silver *denarius*. Caesar's famous and exciting eye-witness account of Britain, the first worthy of the name, was written with a political purpose; it was an apologia, intended to win over public opinion at Rome, since his operations in Gaul and Britain were strictly speaking an illegal private enterprise. Consequently, what he says about Britain must be treated with caution, because he had strong reasons to exaggerate, distort or suppress information. His northern wars provided him with the prestige and the finance which made him 'perpetual dictator', as celebrated here.

'Celtic' British past? Does it stand up to scrutiny? How, at the close of the twentieth century, do scholars see the British Iron Age?

Britons as Celts, and the concept of an Iron Age, are modern interpretations, arising from the work of generations of scholars since the Renaissance. These men were inspired by what they found in surviving Latin and Greek literature.

THE BRITONS THROUGH ROMAN EYES

Until the eighteenth century, almost everything known about Britain before the Roman conquest, such as it was, came from the works of Greco-Roman authors. In the absence of any writings by the Britons themselves, Latin and Greek texts by authors living in the Roman Empire became the sources of the still-familiar stereotypes mentioned above.

There is no known Classical literary work specifically about Britain. The island was always discussed within much larger frameworks of history (e.g., by Caesar, Tacitus and Cassius Dio), of geography (Strabo, Diodorus Siculus) or other literary genres (fig. 3). The surviving texts can be broken into two phases: those based on information available before Caesar's attacks on Britain in 55 and 54 BC; and those written during and after it, when Britain was on the periphery of the Empire and then, from AD 43, undergoing partial conquest.

'Britain was so distant that neither Dionysus nor Herakles went there' (Diodorus Siculus 5,21). These figures travelled the known world in their mythical adventures, the wine-god reaching India, the Hero reaching Gaul; but Britain was so remote that it was almost beyond the reach even of the legends with which the Greeks and Romans explained the universe. This distance, both geographical and cultural, of the Britons from the benchmarks of Greco-Roman civilisation is a persistent theme of these early accounts. Until Caesar, Britain's very existence was doubted by others. A land so literally god-forsaken, set in the midst of awe-inspiring *Oceanus*, the waters which bounded the Earth, was likely to be deeply mysterious and alarming. Even Caesar's hardened legions were jittery at the prospect of crossing to it, while Claudius's invasion force of AD 43 actually mutinied.

After Caesar, Britain became more familiar. For a century it lay on the edge of the Roman Empire, which now stretched to the Channel coast of Gaul. British rulers became trading partners and established diplomatic relations with Rome. From AD 43, substantial parts of the island were conquered, and we have some descriptions of both the provincial population and the tribes beyond the frontiers. From Caesar's accounts, and those which follow, we can piece together a more coherent Roman eye-view of Late Iron Age British societies.

The composite picture of Iron Age Britain, which in recent times has been drawn on the basis of the Classical texts, is of a warlike land of various political units, usually described as tribal states, often fighting each other. Caesar suggests a patchwork of populous and quite wealthy tribal states, which could call on considerable resources. For example the war-leader Cassivellaunus retained 'only' 4,000 chariots for guerrilla warfare against Caesar's army. The named groupings themselves may have been unstable, prone to fragmentation or fusion into larger confederations by alliance or conquest. With the exception of the *Trinovantes* and *Atrebates*, none of the tribes listed by Caesar is certainly attested a century later. This pattern, a complex web of ever-shifting relations running up and down a loosely organised hierarchy of political units, is similar to that which Caesar described in Gaul; some were governed by strong central kings, while others, like Kent, were federations of smaller semi-autonomous units.

Roman accounts concentrate on political and military power, less on other aspects of British life. Britons appeared primitive, without the basics of civilisation as Romans understood them, such as towns and literacy. Caesar describes intensive agriculture in the coastal lands he reconnoitred, but claimed the interior was largely pastoral, and even more barbaric.

Roman authors emphasised those aspects which seemed to them most curious, bizarre, or titillating, not least aspects of religion and the role of women. Britain was said to be the source of Druidism, whose rites so horrified pious Romans – although human sacrifice was occasionally performed in Rome. During the conquest British noblewomen were seen to be directly active in war and politics. Figures like Boudica were bound to attract attention. Caesar records British women with many husbands. Here was further evidence for the barbarian 'otherness' of the British, with the accepted norms of Classical society turned on their heads. Such things could only happen in decadent oriental monarchies like Cleopatra's Egypt, among mythical beings like the Amazons or outlandish barbarians like the British (fig. 4).

What were Roman ideas on the ethnic affiliations of the British? The Romans tended to see many continental peoples as collectively Gauls or Celts, but the British and Irish were consistently seen as separate, even though Caesar and others were well aware of the close contacts across the Channel. In fact, although Roman writers were rather inconsistent in their use of the label 'Celts' – which was most often used as a synonym for 'Gauls' – they were completely consistent in *only* using it for continental peoples, and in *never* using it for the Britons or Irish. There is no sign that they perceived any special characteristics that unified the peoples of Gaul and the peoples of the British Isles, any identity which we might call 'pan-Celtic', which collectively differentiated them from the other dominant North European barbarian group, the Germans.

4 Claudius subdues *Britannia*, a helpless female victim before the might of Roman imperial power personified in the heroic, naked form of the emperor. The figures are identified by a Greek inscription on the separate base slab. Made in the 50s AD this relief, discovered at Aphrodisias in Turkey in 1980, is the earliest-known personification of Britain. It follows a long-established Classical custom of representing cities, peoples and lands in feminine form, as *Fortunae* or goddesses (including *Roma* herself). Britannia was too new an addition to Roman iconography to have evolved any kind of distinctive attributes, such as the trident which she has acquired in Britain in recent centuries.

Caesar recorded that British tribes believed themselves to be indigenous, but had heard that the coastal districts, which were occupied by peoples not unlike the Gauls, had been settled by *Belgae* from Gaul. Tacitus concluded that southern Britain had probably been settled by Gauls in the past, on grounds of similarity of appearance of the peoples, similarity of language and of religion, but he treated Gauls and Britons as ethnically separate.

Britannia, the Roman name for the island, meant 'land of the Britons' – Romans primarily thought in terms of peoples and states, rather than territory. Nevertheless, the Romans were aware of the many political divisions in Britain and of major variations between the populations, eventually distinguishing – albeit vaguely – between *Britanni* in the South, and *Brittones* in the North. In Roman eyes, the Britons were not homogeneous, and not *Celtae*.

In outline, then, Roman views on the Britons seem clear enough.

Yet the texts which survive are few and cursory, a handful of pitiful scraps even for the history of the Roman province. Historians are reduced to inferring imperial intentions, and even the occurrence of entire wars, on the basis of cryptic references in poems. This is hardly a sound basis for attempting to write detailed historical narratives today, yet these sparse remains have long dominated and framed the way scholars look at the period.

Information gleaned from such sources must be used with great caution; they contain obvious difficulties and limitations. Those who actually set foot in Britain, such as Caesar and Tacitus's informant the governor Cn. Julius Agricola, tended to be soldiers on active service, and war is hardly conducive to dispassionate ethnography. Other historians and geographers were writing at second hand, and most never came anywhere near Britain. Their cosmological and geographical views seem strange to us. Romans had an inadequate conception of the shape of Europe – Caesar and Tacitus believed, for example, that Cornwall lay close to Spain.

However, there are also more subtle, yet fundamental difficulties. To assess their value as witnesses for the British Iron Age, we must take into account what these authors were trying to do. History was a branch of literature – style triumphed over content, attention to literary convention over concern for factual accuracy. Roman writers saw no reason even to attempt to achieve objective truth, assuming that is ever possible. Wholly fictitious speeches were put into the mouths of the principal actors, whether Roman or barbarian, and were as much demonstrations of rhetorical skill as evocations of real events. Geographers like Strabo emphasised ethnographic and natural curiosities rather than attempting to understand barbarians on their own terms. Their attitude towards the British was determined by their view of Rome and the Mediterranean as the centre of the world. The distant barbarians of the periphery were expected to exhibit natures appropriate to their place at the edge of outer chaos and darkness. Britons were seen as savages, noble or otherwise, perhaps capable of being 'civilised'.

The surviving accounts also tend to be 'top-down' and very partial. Roman writers were mostly nobles, or at least writing for the nobility, and tended to encounter – and to be most interested in – the upper echelons of British society, mentioning the mass of the people in passing, if at all. Further, they cover only the last quarter of the pre-Roman Iron Age, and only the South.

Consequently, it is clear that the Latin and Greek accounts do not constitute an objective account of the Iron Age, but are more a distorting glass. Because of the long-standing prestige of Classical learning, and until comparatively recently the absence of other information, these perceptions of the Iron Age still widely prevail. They were also the inspiration for the modern definition of a 'Celtic' British past.

Chronological chart, 800 BC – AD 200

	800 BC	700	600	500	400	300	200	100	0	100	AD 200
IRELAND	LATE BRONZE AGE			IRON AGE						ROMAN IRON AGE	
BRITAIN	LATE BRONZE AGE		EARLY IRON AGE		MIDDLE IRON AGE			LATE IRON AGE		ROMAN IRON AGE / ROMAN	
FRANCE (GAUL)	FINAL BRONZE AGE / URNFIELDS	HALLSTATT I	HALLSTATT II		LA TÈNE I — a b c		LA TÈNE II — a b	LA TÈNE III		ROMAN	
SOUTHERN GERMANY	HALLSTATT B	HALLSTATT C	HALLSTATT D — 1 2 3		LA TÈNE A	LA TÈNE B — 1 2	LA TÈNE C — 1 2	LA TÈNE D — 1 2	ROMAN		
CENTRAL ITALY	VILLANOVAN		ETRUSCAN CITY STATES		LATINS			R O M A N			
GREECE	GEOMETRIC		ARCHAIC	CLASSICAL			HELLENISTIC		ROMAN		
NEAR EAST	ASSYRIAN			ACHAEMENID / PERSIAN			HELLENISTIC		ROMAN / PARTHIAN		
CHINA	CHOU DYNASTY			WARRING STATES				CH'IN	HAN DYNASTY		

Annotations on chart:
Lindow Man, *Boudica*, *Snettisham Hoards*, *East Yorkshire Cemeteries*, *Deal Warrior*, *Maiden Castle hill fort*, *Julius Caesar*, *Alexander*

THE REINVENTION OF THE 'CELTS'

As they glimpsed their forgotten ancestors in the pages of Caesar and Tacitus, scholars of the Renaissance states of France and the British Isles began to be interested in these earliest attested peoples of their own lands. Given the primacy of the written word, it is not surprising that early speculations were primarily historical and linguistic – archaeology developed later.

In 1703, the Breton Abbé Pezron published a book which, on the basis of evidence for languages ancient and modern, suggested that the Ancient British were the same as the *Celtae* or *Galli* (Gauls) of France. This was received with enthusiasm by the Welsh scholar Edward Lhuyd who, in 1707, published his own influential work which proposed that Welsh, Breton, Irish and Scots Gaelic and their ancestral tongues were all related to the ancient Gaulish language. It was a major breakthrough. He chose to call this family of languages 'Celtic'. Insular 'Celtic speakers' were soon being called 'Celts' as an ethnic label. This was the route whereby the notion that people in the British Isles are 'Celtic' became established during the eighteenth century, leading directly to the use of the term by cultural and nationalist movements of recent times, and to the retrospective labelling of the Ancient British and Irish as Celts. As archaeological remains began to be identified, they were interpreted in terms of this predefined historical and cultural framework. In England, the anti-quary William Stukeley was calling ancient monuments 'Celtic' as early as 1723. Thereafter, various aspects of ancient material culture, and especially certain artistic styles, came to be labelled 'Celtic' too.

ARCHAEOLOGY DEFINES THE IRON AGE

Pre-Roman objects, including artefacts such as coins that would later be identified as belonging to the last centuries BC, were accumulating in British and Continental collections during the eighteenth and nineteenth centuries. The problems were to establish how old these objects were, and to relate them to historically-attested peoples.

The discovery that the history of the world was to be measured in millions of years rather than a few thousand led to the realisation that there were vast swathes of pre-historic time, i.e. time before the first surviving documents. The recognition of human-made tools from these periods led to the division of human prehistory according to the 'Three Age System' of successive eras defined by the dominant toolmaking material of each: stone, bronze and iron. The archaeological idea of an Iron Age was suggested by the Dane C. J. Thomsen in a book of 1836.

The key to unravelling the nature and chronology of later prehistory also came from the Continent (fig. 5). In the case of the Iron Age,

5 The archaeological chronologies of Iron Age Britain, its neighbours and, for comparison, some of the great civilisations of the Mediterranean and Asia. (Based on Collis, 1984, fig. 2 and other sources). The British chronology was originally worked out in relation to the Continental Hallstatt and La Tène chronologies, which were themselves linked to the more detailed chronologies of the Classical world. Diagrams like these, necessary though they are, may give a misleading impression of precision and finality. Yet archaeological dating remains generally 'fuzzy' and imprecise even today, and of course the phases of development defined and labelled here did not actually have such sharp edges; the divisions are more approximate, and less certain, than the sharp lines imply. Some are in the process of substantial revision; for example, the German chronology now divides the La Tène D1 and D2 phases into a and b subphases, and this scheme has generally replaced the French La Tène I to III scheme among Northern French archaeologists. Meanwhile, the start of the British Iron Age now looks to be pushing back towards the eighth century BC. If this is so, then it is likely that the continental chronologies will need to be pushed earlier, too.

6 Sequencing the British Iron Age, 1: Fibulae (bow-brooches)

Fibulae are the most common artefact-type in burials and settlements throughout much of continental Europe so their evolution from the eighth to the first centuries BC can be used to produce a relative framework into which other artefacts can be slotted. British finds do not conform to the pattern on the continent, particularly during the Hallstatt C period when there is a marked shortage of finds. Fibulae did not entirely replace pins for fastening clothing until the third century BC.

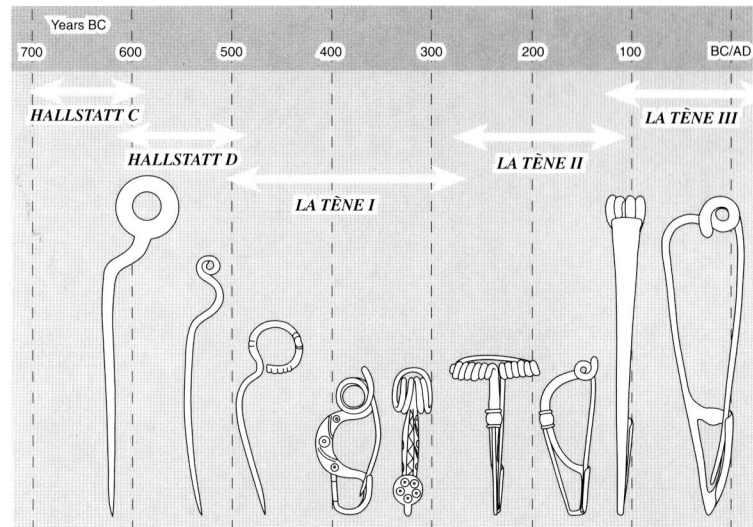

7 Sequencing the British Iron Age, 2: Swords and Scabbards

Marked changes occurred in the size and shape of iron swords in the Hallstatt and La Tène Iron Ages, which must be due to different ways of fighting as well as manufacturing techniques. Only two iron swords of Hallstatt C have been found in Britain, raising the question of what weapons were used between 750 BC, the revised date for the end of the Late Bronze Age, and 600 BC, the conventional date for the beginning of Hallstatt D, when finds of daggers or short swords are comparatively common. Hallstatt D and La Tène I daggers or short swords are similar in shape, size and style to continental examples, the main distinguishing feature being the suspension loop which is formed by two separate iron wires.

In the La Tène period metal scabbards were highly prized and skilled smiths produced outstanding decorative effects on the front plate, chape and even the suspension-loop on the back. The altered position of the latter demonstrates that the way in which the scabbard was worn changed radically.

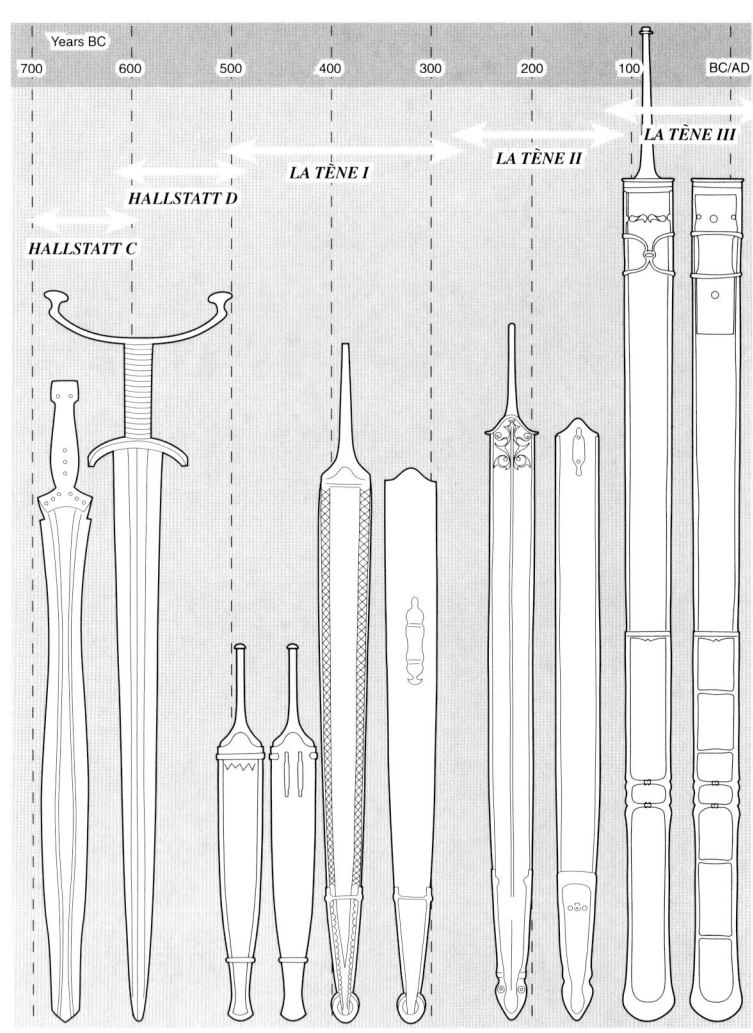

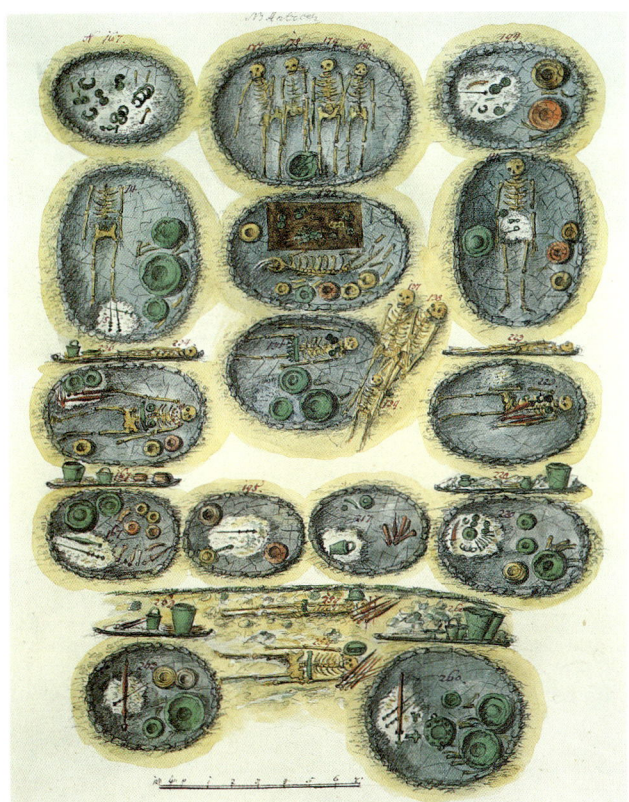

8 *above* Some of the inhumation and cremation graves from the great cemetery at Hallstatt in Austria, the 'type-site' for the Hallstatt Culture. Ramsauer recorded his excavations meticulously, producing fine watercolour sketches of the grave layouts, and the objects in them.

9 *above right* Vehicle-grave found at Somme-Bionne, near Châlons-sur-Marne, France. Early finds like this helped to sort out the chronology of later prehistory north of the Alps, because in addition to locally-made items, the grave contained imports from the Classical world, a two-handled Greek drinking cup and an Etruscan flagon. The cup was of quite accurately known date, made *c.* 420 BC, and it is unlikely to have been very old when buried. The flagon is also consistent with burial *c.* 400 BC. Such finds allowed approximate linkage of the undated Northern sequences of artistic and cultural development with those of the Classical world, where the chronologies of pottery and metalwork were already well understood. Nevertheless, dating of finds often remains very approximate, although newer scientific techniques such as radiocarbon analysis and dendrochronology (tree-ring dating) are gradually refining the picture.

this was especially from Ramsauer's excavations (1846–62) of the spectacular cemeteries at Hallstatt, in Austria, where rich grave offerings included Italian imports which could be related to the better-known archaeology of the Classical world (fig. 8). These, and the discoveries of decorated swords and other objects in the lake-bed at La Tène, Switzerland, in 1858, led by the 1870s to the definition of two successive Iron Age cultures in Europe: the earlier Hallstatt Culture, and the later La Tène culture (figs. 5–7). Spectacular burials attributable to the La Tène culture, including chariot graves with datable Greek imports, were found in France and Germany (fig. 9). Here were traces of peoples who could plausibly be identified as the Celts or Gauls of the Greek and Latin texts. But for most of Britain there were no comparable Iron Age graves with offerings for the early antiquaries to discover. Nevertheless there were chance discoveries, not least river-finds like the Thames 'helmet' and the Battersea shield, with decoration intimately related to the characteristic art of the La Tène culture (figs. 26 and 12). The archaeology of Britain was clearly similar to that of ancient Gaul, but far from identical. How were they connected?

Archaeological remains cannot be linked unequivocally with ethnic groups known from documentary sources, unless they have comprehensible texts written on them – something absent in prehistory

by definition. Archaeologists seek to link 'mute' artefacts to other objects from known periods or places, through similarity of form, decorative style or other properties. This helps to place them in time, and in relation to known archaeological 'cultures'. People then attempt to interpret these 'cultures' in terms of the historical and ethnic categories known to them – not least the Celts (fig. 10). Finds of La Tène-style objects in Britain might, then, imply Celtic invaders from the Continent.

In 1886 Arthur Evans' discovery of a cremation cemetery at Aylesford, Kent, was followed by related finds from Welwyn, Hertfordshire, and Swarling, Kent (fig. 11 and front cover). Clearly related to Gaulish burial rites, these graves were seen as evidence for Caesar's Belgic settlers. Such finds, and the growing belief in the immigrant nature of the 'Arras culture' represented by the cemeteries of East Yorkshire (p. 67), encouraged the idea of invasion as the principal, even sole, cause of change in prehistoric Britain.

10 *above* Augustus Wollaston Franks, pioneer of the prehistoric collections at the British Museum where, in 1863, illustrating a series of prehistoric objects which we would now assign to the La Tène culture, 'he was forced to refer to them as 'Late Keltic' for want of a more precise terminology' (Cunliffe, 1994, 1–2).

11 *right* Finds from a cremation in the Aylesford Cemetery, outside Maidstone, Kent, recovered during quarrying in 1886. It was the subject of the first systematic study of Late Iron Age cremation burial, 'On a Late-Celtic Urn-Field at Aylesford Kent…' by Arthur Evans, who fully understood the significance of the continental origins of many of the grave goods. It later became the type-site for the 'Aylesford Culture'. This particular grave excited great interest because of the splendid decoration of the bucket which contained the cremation and two bronze brooches. About 50 BC. H. of bucket 300 mm.

12 *opposite page* Important early finds from the river Thames, including the Battersea shield, illustrated in John A. Kemble's *Horae Ferales* (1868). Edited and published after Kemble's death by R. G. Latham and A. W. Franks, the volume featured accurate and detailed illustrations of British and continental artefacts, many, like these, already in the collections of the British Museum. It was instrumental in defining the British Iron Age.

PLATE XV

Scale 2/7 linear.

O. Jewitt, lith.

Vincent Brooks, Imp.

SHIELD AND SWORD FROM THE THAMES.

In 1930–1 Christopher Hawkes, then an Assistant Keeper at the British Museum, was inspired largely by his work on the Museum's collections to define several hypothetical waves of invaders to explain the successive changes seen in the archaeology. This became the Iron Age A, B and C scheme, the basis for research for the next thirty years. This invasion theory fitted well with prevailing assumptions of early Celts migrating from a supposed Central European homeland, carrying their characteristic art and metalwork with them.

Subsequently, the ABC scheme became increasingly complicated by local and chronological subdivisions, as more and more pot types and other variant archaeological forms appeared to demand yet further waves of invaders. However, there was a growing realisation of a lack of clear evidence for substantial migrations from the Continent; where were the imported objects, foreign-style burial rites or settlements? Apart from the localised 'Arras Culture' and 'Aylesford Culture', there was little plausible sign of immigration. It was becoming clear from anthropology that non-industrial societies experience far more internal change than had been assumed, and so invasions were not necessary to explain all major developments in the archaeological record. Indeed, it was increasingly evident that much that characterised the British Iron Age could be traced to roots in the local Bronze Age, rather than to the Continent.

In 1964, Roy Hodson suggested the idea of an indigenous British 'Woodbury Culture' growing out of the Bronze Age, with intrusive 'Aylesford Culture' (fig. 11) and 'Arras Culture'. Emphasis was now placed on continuity from earlier times, with varying degrees of continental cultural contact. For example, Iron Age British metalwork is closely related to the continental La Tène tradition, but is stylistically distinctive, and used in different ways. This connection is best explained through mechanisms such as trade and exchange. Although some localised episodes of migration and settlement remain probable, invasion has long been out of favour as the main explanation. Nevertheless, the idea that Britain was part of a wider Celtic *cultural* world remains important. This is the framework of understanding which the current generation of archaeologists has inherited.

What follows is an archaeology-led survey of what we know about Britons and their world, and what we conclude from it about their relations with their continental Celtic neighbours, starting with a look at the people themselves.

2 The people

In the absence of any pre-Roman artefact bearing a naturalistic portrait of an individual, our earliest detailed portrayal of Britons comes from the writings of Julius Caesar, although as we have seen such sources cannot be taken at face value. Caesar accurately described Britain as a populous land, but his distinction between aboriginal inhabitants of the interior who wore skins and herded animals, and recent immigrants on the coast who live a more 'civilised' life like their Gaulish neighbours, is at least a grave oversimplification. Nevertheless, he records that males wore their hair long and sported moustaches. Shaving their bodies, they painted themselves with a blue pigment. Women did not warrant even these brief details; it was left to Cassius Dio much later to describe Boudica as tall, tawny-haired, wearing long flowing garments and a gold necklet. However, this may be a stock Classical description for any prominent barbarian woman – Briton, Gaul or German – living north of the Mediterranean world. Archaeology allows us to gain a rather firmer, if still highly fragmentary, picture of what Britons were physically like, from surviving human remains.

FINDING THE PEOPLE

Physical remains of Iron Age Britons themselves are elusive. During the first millennium BC, the great majority of the bodies of the millions of people who lived out their days on the island appear to have been disposed of in ways which have left no archaeological traces. Even in the limited areas and periods where there are cemeteries, our exploration of the surviving evidence is still at a rudimentary stage, but fascinating results are already emerging.

Detailed study of human remains by palaeopathologists provides information about an individual's appearance, health, lifespan and, sometimes, cause of death. Only when skeletons are well preserved is it possible to distinguish male from female, or estimate height and detect abnormalities with any precision. Typically in any cemetery fewer than half the bodies are sufficiently complete to provide reliable data. Studies of skeletons excavated from cemeteries in East Yorkshire and Kent, and remains found inside Danebury hillfort, Hampshire, provide some statistical information about local populations which illustrates something of the diversity of the peoples of Britain. The discovery of bog bodies at Lindow Moss, Cheshire has, literally and metaphorically, added flesh to these bare bones.

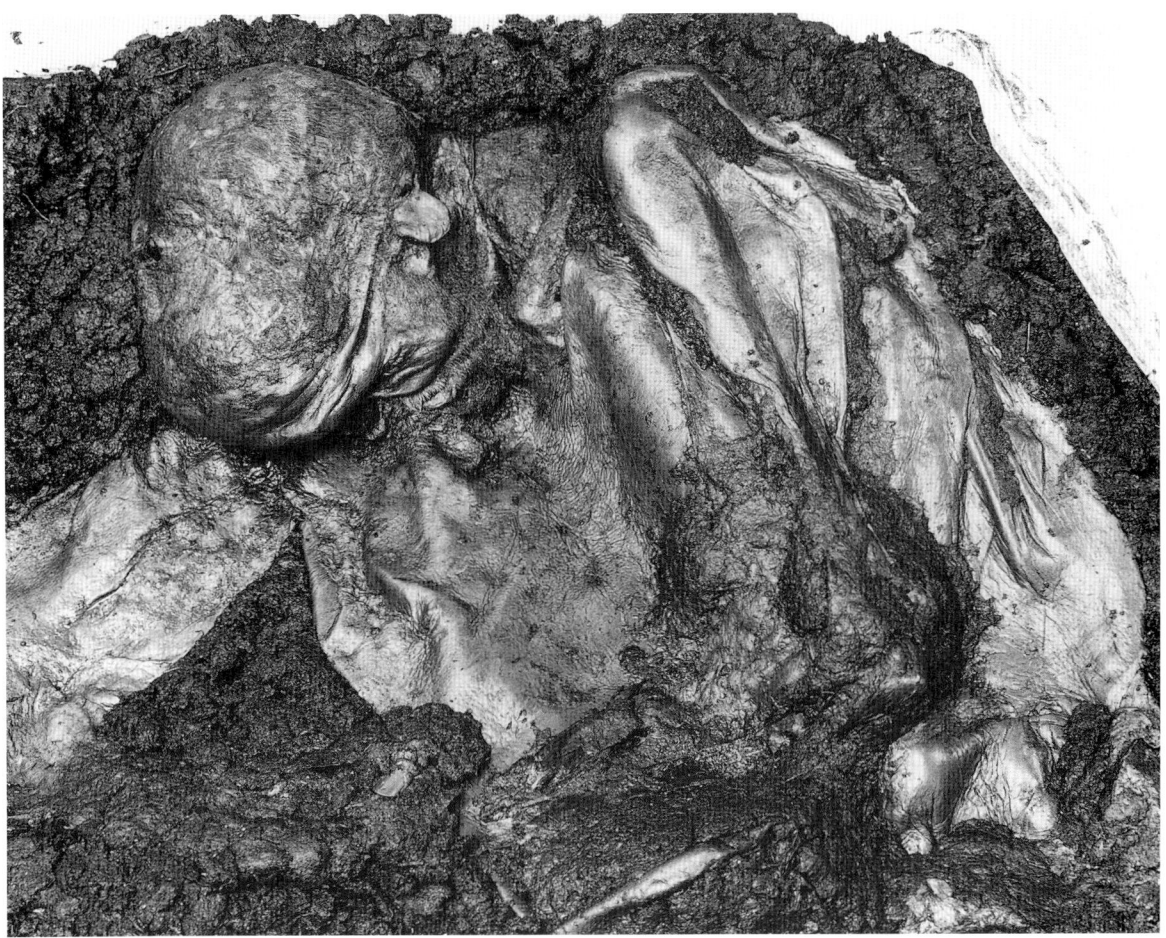

14 Lindow Man or 'Pete Marsh', more formally known as Lindow II, after excavation. The ligature around his neck is just visible. When discovered he was face down in peat in what had originally been a shallow pool.

APPEARANCE

Lindow Man, a bog body discovered in 1984, allows us to construct a compelling picture of a Briton (fig. 14). Nicknamed 'Pete Marsh', he is officially called Lindow II since a skull (Lindow I) and a fragmented headless body (Lindow III) have also been found at the same place, Lindow Moss, Cheshire. Permanent immersion in the oxygen-free and biologically sterile waters of the bog meant that, besides bone, his skin, hair and much soft tissue survived, providing specialists with evidence of appearance, musculature, nutrition and health not available from skeletons alone. Killed at around the age of 25, he stood about 1.69 m tall (5'6"), was heavily built and well-muscled with no congenital deformities. It has proved more difficult to say exactly when he lived: in the absence of any datable artefacts with the body, we must rely on scientific measurements of weak, natural radioactivity in his tissues and the surrounding peat. Unfortunately, the results are confused and contradictory in detail, but do point to a date of death in the later Iron Age, or perhaps the very beginning of the Roman period.

The forensic reconstruction of his head reproduces his Caucasoid features, short straight hair, neatly trimmed moustache and beard (fig. 15). The colouring of skin and eyes is conjectural, although its composition suggests his hair was dark. Just such a full-bearded face is pictured on a bronze coin struck in the early first century AD (fig. 16). Mature moustachioed males with clean-shaven chin are depicted on the three miniature masks found at Welwyn, Hertfordshire (fig. 17). In contrast, the youthful face incorporated in the bronze pommel of an iron sword is clean shaven with swept back hair arranged in a pig-tail or bun (fig. 18). No comparable artefact portrays a woman.

Can Lindow Man be taken as a typical, indigenous Iron Age Briton? Probably, but the possibility that he was an incomer cannot be excluded.

STATURE AND STATUS

To discuss populations, we need more bodies to provide statistical data. Substantial groups of skeletons are known only from a few areas and periods where local traditions or fashions for formal burials

15 *right* Suggested reconstruction of the head of Lindow II by Richard Neave. As it survives his hair is light auburn, but further investigation suggested that acid ground water destroyed the natural brown hair pigment (eumelanin), leaving him as a bleached red-head although in life his hair was dark brown. High magnification demonstrates that his beard and hair had been trimmed with shears rather than a razor.

Opposite page
16 *top* Obverse of a bronze coin depicting the full-bearded face of an unknown man of high status. It is inscribed TASC for Tasciovanus (a leader of the *Catuvellauni* after Caesar's campaigns) and was minted some time between AD 5 and 40.
17 *centre* A cast bronze mask depicting a mature moustachioed male found in a rich cremation burial dating to the period *c.* 50–20 BC at Welwyn, Hertfordshire, on the boundary of two major tribes of the time, the *Trinovantes* and the *Catuvellauni*. L. 39 mm.
18 *bottom* The cast bronze anthropoid hilt of an iron sword found in a burial at North Grimston, East Yorkshire, and dated to the second century BC. The pommel is in the form of a human head modelled in the round. The face is youthful and clean-shaven with the hair drawn back from the forehead in stylised waves but straight at the back. Human figures were not portrayed in any way in the early British Iron Age so that, although the face is not an individual portrait, it is one of the earliest recognisable human representations yet found in Britain. H. of head 28 mm.

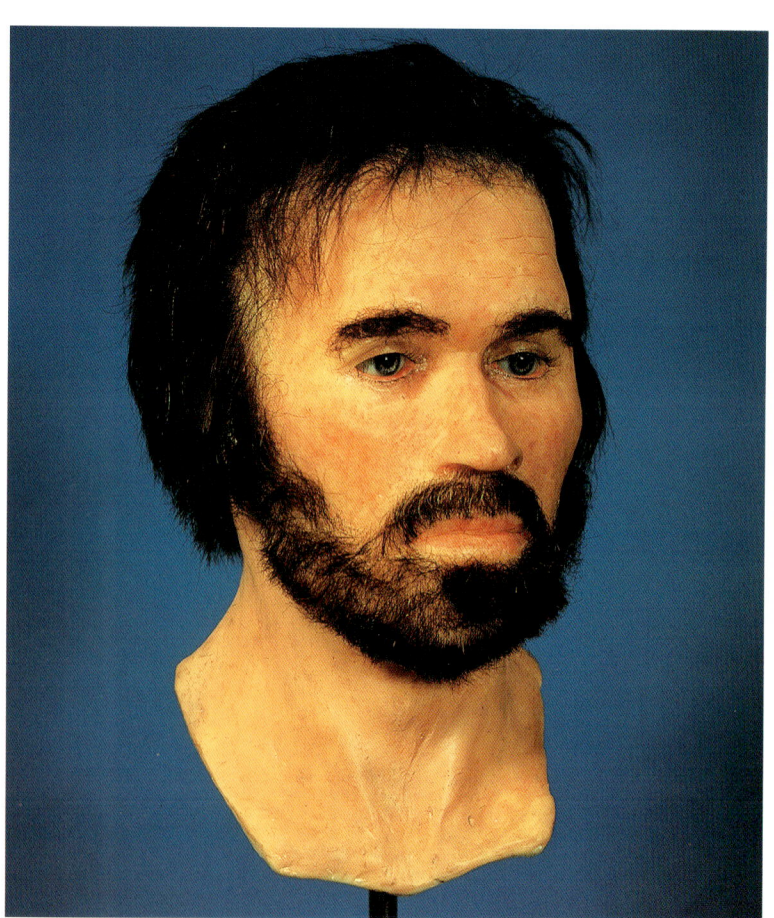

19 *right* One of a pair of cast bronze handle mounts depicting a head wearing a helmet or headdress surmounted by a pair of twisted ram's horns. The delicate features are in marked contrast to those of the Aylesford bucket mount and may be those of a woman rather than a youth. The wooden bucket was encased in bronze bands and it formed part of a burial group excavated at Alkham, Kent. Mid-first century BC. H. 42 mm.

in cemeteries became established, or where human remains were often buried in 'domestic' contexts like pits. These include the cemeteries of Rudston, Burton Fleming, Garton Station and Kirkburn, in East Yorkshire and Deal, Kent and the skeletal material from Maiden Castle and Poundbury, Dorset, and Danebury, Hampshire.

From this data, average stature of adult males has been calculated to 1.69 m (5′6½″), roughly Lindow Man's height. Averages obscure potentially significant differences; the range is 1.6 m to 1.8 m (5′2″–5′11″). As is usual among human populations, women were shorter, average height being 1.5 m (5′2″) and the range 1.4–1.7 m (4′9″–5′7″). To rank as tall Boudica should have equalled the tallest females in the population who were 1.6 m (5′4″) at Deal (shorter than the male average), but 1.7 m (5′7″) at Garton Station, about the height of an average male and taller than Lindow Man.

In the Garton Station and Kirkburn cemeteries, East Yorkshire, both males and females were taller than these averages. The sample is small and so may be unrepresentative, but one explanation of their greater stature is that they enjoyed superior diet due to high social status. They were probably community leaders and so enjoyed the advantages of a better lifestyle and nutrition, particularly when young. A radical alternative is that they belonged to a separate ethnic group which was genetically taller than the rest of the population.

There is no doubt, however, that at 1.6 m (5′4″) the Deal Warrior has to be classed as short and slight (fig. 24). He is the only individual buried with a sword in the Iron Age inhumation cemetery excavated at Deal, Kent. His grave goods are amongst the most spectacular of any British burial and he demonstrates that in the third century BC, in his community at least, status was not automatically tied to stature.

If the age-at-death estimates for people buried in the Yorkshire and Deal cemeteries are correct, few adults survived to 50 years. The death-rate of children below the age of 15 shows no particular peaks suggesting that, as expected among populations without benefit of modern medicine, birth presented the greatest danger and children surviving infancy then had a reasonable life-expectancy. The risks of child-birth to young women of child-bearing age, 17–25 years, appear to have outweighed that of active, accident-prone young males. At Kirkburn two women had died in child-birth. They were buried in the same grave with a full-term and a new-born infant. These were the only babies excavated. There were certainly many more deaths than this in infancy, when children were at their most vulnerable to infection. Younger children must usually have been buried elsewhere.

The picture presented by skeletons buried in pits within the defences of the Danebury Hillfort, Hampshire, is very different. Here the expected levels of infant mortality are attested; a quarter of children died before the age of two years. Theoretically, with increasing age the chances of survival improve but at Danebury surprisingly high numbers of children died between the ages of 8 and 12 years.

At Danebury the overall number of dead males is more than twice that of females, which, as with Yorkshire's missing infants, probably reflects how the dead were selected for particular burial rites rather than the true demographic structure. There are other differences. No deformities due to prolonged dietary deficiency in infancy were detected in the formal cemeteries, but at Danebury there is skeletal degeneration thought to be due to iron deficiency or anaemia in up to 50 per cent of children and 25 per cent of adults. It may reflect a deficiency in Vitamin C, necessary to metabolise iron, rather than the lack of iron itself. At Danebury many people suffered poor health.

Besides diet, longevity is affected by genetics, infectious disease and violence. In the Yorkshire cemeteries no major congenital abnormalities were detected, perhaps implying infanticide of obviously deformed or sickly babies. Most infectious diseases affect soft tissue only, leaving little effect on the skeletal frame. Debilitating parasitic infestations, related to poor hygiene, probably afflicted many people. Lindow Man was plagued by round-worms. One case of atrophy of lower leg-bones at Rudston was ascribed to polio, otherwise there are cases of malignant and benign bone tumours. Arthritis of the spine was by far the most common of several chronic degenerative conditions. At least a quarter of the population suffered serious back trouble, evidence of a strenuous life. Long hours spent squatting at unidentified tasks affected women's leg joints at Deal and Danebury. Teeth were troublesome, and generally women's oral health was

20 A fragment of textile preserved wrapped round an iron brooch found behind the neck of a male skeleton in a grave at Burton Fleming, North Humberside. Originally part of a cloak or stole, it survived because the threads in contact with the brooch became impregnated with iron corrosion before they could perish. Third or second century BC. L. from selvedge 28 mm.

worse than men's, probably the result of calcium deficiency due to the effects of pregnancies.

Infected wounds could prove life-threatening. Some time before death the Deal Warrior suffered a serious spinal wound which perhaps became infected, producing an abnormality in the healed area. Considering that sixteen males went to the grave at Rudston–Burton Fleming armed with swords and spears it is perhaps surprising that here there is little evidence of weapon injury. Five males did, however, have healed collar-bone fractures, injuries typical of falls when riding or driving horses. In contrast, at Danebury wounds from edged weapons were recorded on fifteen out of ninety-five burials; in thirteen of these cases death occurred soon after wounding, as healing had not begun.

Our anatomical picture of Britons, then, is extremely fragmentary, and far from representative of the population of the island as a whole. Such evidence we have shows considerable variation, but is generally consistent with other 'pre-medical' societies.

COSTUME

Careful excavation of inhumation burials provides the only secure information about the costume of Britons, since there are no unambiguous depictions pre-dating AD 43, nor any detailed contemporary descriptions. Inference rests chiefly on tiny fragments of woollen fabric, or textile impressions wrapped around corroded iron artefacts which have been painstakingly studied by specialists. Almost nothing survives of the shape, cut and fastening of garments, or sewing techniques.

The most informative fragment is embroidery wrapped round a long iron brooch dating to the second century BC in the grave of a male in East Yorkshire (figs. 20 and 21). It was part of a rectangular cloak, stole

21 Reconstruction of the pattern forming the border of the cloak or stole. As restored from thirteen small fragments it comprises a wide continuous band, with stripes of different colours and embroidered details, around two adjoining sides of a rectangular piece of twill-woven wool. Twill weave is used for patterns based on diagonal stripes, including diamonds and dog-tooth check effects, and also produces an extra-warm fabric of double thickness.

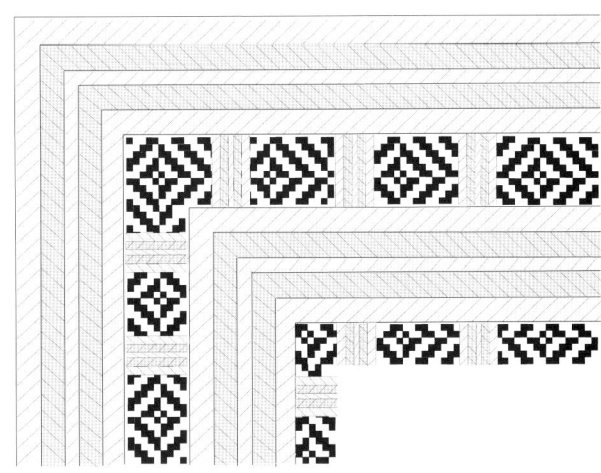

or shroud presumably draped around the shoulders and fastened there with a single side opening allowing freedom to one arm. The garment could also have been worn draped over the head and fastened below the chin for in some graves the fastener lies below the jaw. Other fragments illustrate the survival of decorative fringes left when the warp threads of the textile were cut from the loom.

The only fasteners to be found *in situ* in burials are single ring-headed pins and bow brooches, usually of iron, lying near the shoulder of both females and males where they functioned as modern safety-pins. Ring-headed pins, in bronze and later in iron, evolved in Britain in the eighth century BC (fig. 22). Something can be inferred about clothing from their shape and chronological evolution. The angled shank allows several thicknesses of fabric to be pleated or gathered, while the ring can be threaded with cord, tassels or braids to heighten the decorative effect. By the third century BC pins were replaced by bow brooches which were more secure and comfortable to wear. Early brooches with high, humped bows allowed several thicknesses of drapery to be secured. They were in turn superseded by variants with a flattened bow for simple flat-pinning of cloth with no pleats or gathers, which must reflect some change in the appearance of the garment.

None of the ornaments recovered from East Yorkshire burials suggest a flamboyant style of dress while little survives to distinguish female from male. Females occasionally wear a pair of bangles at the wrist possibly securing the long sleeves of a tunic or gown, and even more rarely there are necklaces of glass beads. Single beads found at the back of the skull may have been worn as earrings or hair ornaments. Both sexes occasionally wore finger- or toe-rings. Bright and permanent colour is produced by a stud of coral or opaque red glass

22 Swan's neck, ring-headed and involuted pins in bronze and iron were used to secure a cloak or stole at the shoulder. The globular head of one is ornamented with coral insets. Eighth–third century BC. L. of longest pin 125 mm.

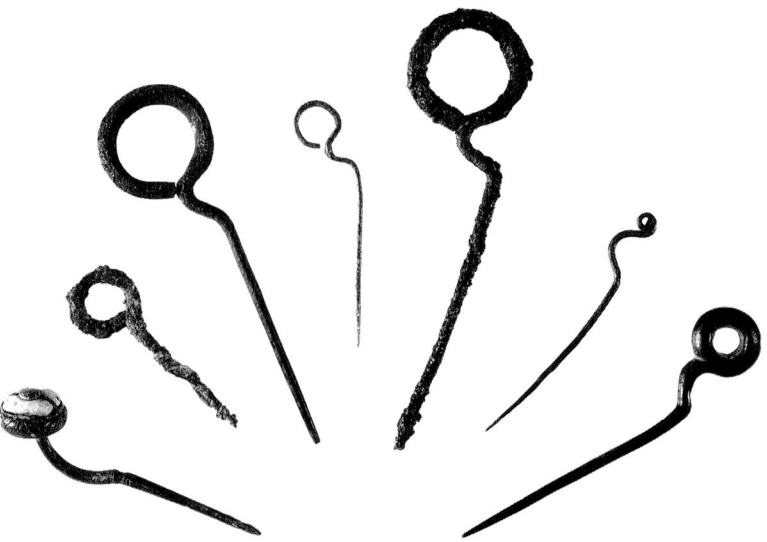

23 A selection of jewellery worn by women and girls in the fourth and third centuries BC. Bronze brooches and bracelets were inlaid with studs of red and white coral and opaque red glass; alongside necklaces of blue and white glass beads they added spots of bright and permanent colour to costume, but they cannot be described as flamboyant and the brooches were functional. Diam. of bronze bangles about 60 mm.

on a brooch or bangle and by bead necklaces chiefly in blue and blue with white inlay (fig. 23).

Grave goods in southern British cremation burials of the first century BC and AD give a glimpse of a change in costume and a more luxurious and colourful life-style. Pairs of long slender bow-brooches in silver, joined by lengths of chain, imply that the outer garment now had a central opening and was flat pinned, not draped. Fragments of cloth of gold, and fabric decorated with silver appliqués imported from the eastern Mediterranean or beyond and used either as either garments or hangings, survived in the Lexden Tumulus. This was the resting place of a man of wealth and high status buried outside the *oppidum* at Colchester, Essex, in the late first century BC. Fur may have been worn: at least two bodies were wrapped in bearskins before being cremated and buried at Welwyn Garden City and Baldock, Hertfordshire. Lindow Man certainly wore a fox fur armband.

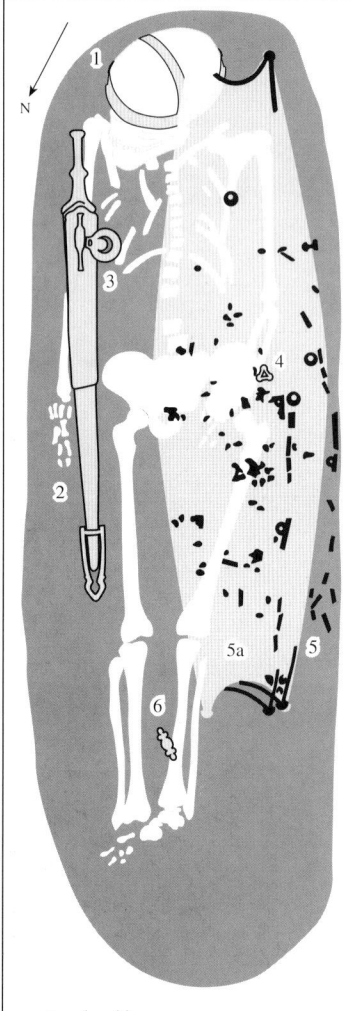

1 headdress
2 sword
3–4 sword attachments
4 shield (fragments)
5a shield (reconstructed shape)
5 shield (reconstructed shape)
6 brooch

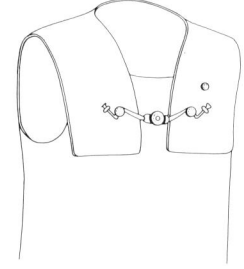

ARMS, REGALIA AND DISPLAY

Evidence for male personal adornment has a strong military aspect. Both Lindow Man (Lindow II) and the fragmented Lindow III were naked when deposited in the peat-bog. They may confirm the eye-witness claim of Caesar that some British warriors opposing his landing in 55 BC fought naked, and had painted their bodies blue with the pigment *vitrum*. Traces of copper compounds apparently detected on the torso of Lindow II could be the remains of a blue body paint and evidence that a metallic compound was used, not the vegetable dye woad. However, some researchers consider the traces represent chemical contamination while the body was buried in peat.

Not all warriors went naked into battle. The body buried with a dismantled vehicle at Kirkburn in the third century BC was accompanied by a thigh-length shirt of iron chain mail (fig. 25). Few males were buried with such ornamented weaponry as the Kirkburn and Deal Warriors (fig. 24). Spears, or occasionally a shield are more common.

While warrior symbolism was important, religious or political status was also represented in dress. The two-horned 'helmet' dredged from the Thames near Waterloo Bridge would provide little protection and is more likely to be a ceremonial head-dress (fig. 26), as is the 'crown', made of decorated bronze strips, worn by the Deal Warrior (fig. 27).

In the first century BC, evidence of conspicuous display is represented by numerous massive, shining torcs or neck-rings in gold, silver and bronze which have been found in hoards. Their flexibility shows that they could have been worn, but none has been found in a grave or depicted in statuary. Only one possible instance of torc-wearing has been recorded: when Boudica led an army against the Romans in AD 60/1 (p. 16). Perhaps in Britain at that time gold was used to proclaim leadership.

THE AFFILIATIONS OF THE BRITISH

What can be said of the biological and cultural affiliations of the Britons from surviving bodies and cemeteries? We cannot yet compare Gauls and Britons from skeletal remains, due to the sparseness and unevenness of biological data, and controversy over scientific methods. Within Britain, the evidence suggests important variations

24 *top* Warrior burial found in an Iron Age cemetery at Mill Hill, Deal, Kent. The body was laid directly in the grave without a coffin. Made of leather-covered wood with bronze binding and boss, the shield can be reconstructed into a shape which is also attested elsewhere, and appears to be uniquely British. Late third to early second century BC.

25 *left* A reconstruction of the tunic made of iron chain-mail found folded at the feet of the skeleton in a vehicle-burial at Kirkburn, East Yorkshire. In all perhaps 5,000 rings were required. Third century BC.

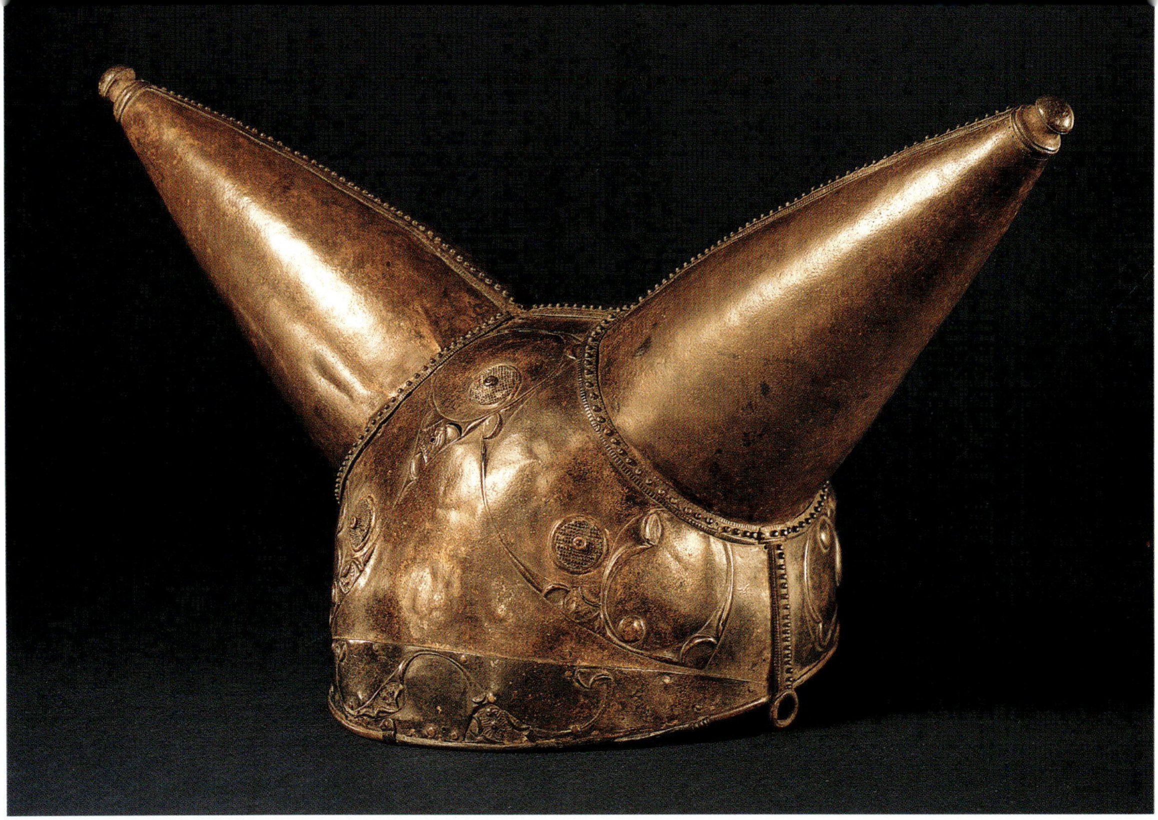

26 *above* The back view of a 'helmet' dredged from the Thames at Waterloo Bridge and dated on stylistic grounds to the first century BC. It is made of riveted sheet-bronze components. The relief ornament is repeated on the front and highlighted with studs of opaque red glass. It is probably a symbolic headdress like that depicted on the Alkham bucket mounts. H. 242 mm.

27 *right* The bronze 'crown' or head-dress as found on the skull of the Deal warrior. The engraved decoration is repeated around the head-band but the cross-band is plain. Human hair was found in corrosion on the inner surface showing that the metal was not padded or strengthened with leather. Late third to early second century BC.

28 The Snettisham 'Great Torc' is perhaps the finest of its kind yet found. Undoubtedly it was made to impress observers, whether its precise function was to be worn regularly as an ornament or badge of office, or simply to be placed on display. The 'Great Torc' is far larger and more conspicuous than most jewellery worn during the British Iron Age. The hoop is made of eight hollow spiral strands each composed of eight wires spiralled together to form a hollow tube. The hollow ring terminals are decorated in relief enhanced with engraved texture. Use of hollow components maximised the overall size of the torc for the weight of gold employed. About 70 BC. Diam. 199 mm.

between relatively tiny samples of people from Yorkshire, Hampshire and Kent , but as we have seen these may be reflecting differing social ranks, rather than major genetic differences.

However, it is interesting that the Classical texts suggest Romans perceived regional population differences within Britain. If based on observation – and they do correspond with more recent British national stereotypes – descriptions of tall, fair, southern Britons, red-haired Caledonians, and swarthy *Silures* (South Wales) suggest biological, as well as cultural, diversity, and a long and complex demographic history. Southern Britons were not clearly distinguished from the Gauls, who were also stereotyped as tall and fair – but then so were the Germans. At least, all this emphasises that there was no simple equation of racial type and 'Celtic' culture.

Evidence for dress and display certainly reveals links with continental Europe, for example through adoption of Gallic brooch-types. Yet equally, important categories of adornment such as ring-headed pins show the continuity of local traditions. Use of torcs was shared with the Gauls, but they were worn by non-Celtic peoples as well.

The implications of this evidence, and that of burial rites, for the question of 'Celticity' and possible Celtic immigration, are discussed in Chapters 5 and 6.

3 Making a living

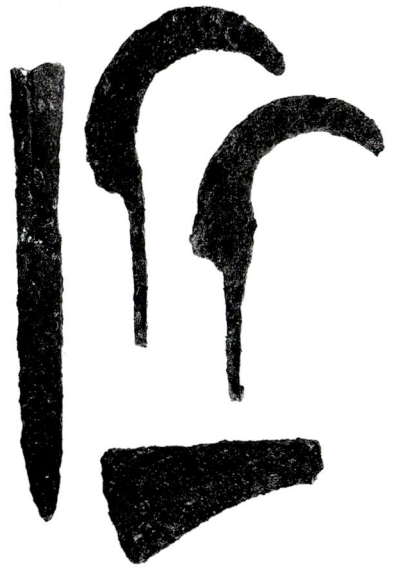

For the Classical world, information about the fundamentals of daily life is provided by both archaeology, and by surviving texts. For example, Pliny's *Natural History* provides immense detail on the occupations, crafts and arts of the Roman world, while Apicius collected recipes which give a glimpse of the domestic arrangements of the rich. Lacking a comparable documentary record, prehistorians work by deduction from the context and detailed examination of surviving artefacts, and use ideas and observations from social anthropology and ethnographic studies, combined with experiments to replicate objects and processes.

To subsist satisfactorily, a community needed adequate water and food, and free local access to as many raw materials as possible for shelter, clothing and equipment. Some, such as timber or clay, were usually easily at hand. Others, notably metal ores, were much more localised, and so were often beyond the control of many communities; metal had to be acquired by exchange. Networks established in the Bronze Age, connecting Britain to the Baltic and Aegean, redistributed raw materials, particularly copper, tin and lead. Purely decorative substances like amber and coral were also imported. Kimmeridge shale for beads and bangles, quarried on the Isle of Purbeck, Dorset, became one of the most widely distributed materials in Britain.

THE FRUITS OF THE LAND: FOOD AND DIET

Animal husbandry and cereal growing, adopted in Britain some 3,000 years earlier, were intensified from 500 BC with more and larger settlements and extension of enclosed field systems. The change from bronze to iron for farming implements led to a more effective ard (simple scratch-plough; fig. 29). Sometime after 150 BC ox-drawn ploughs were introduced into parts of southern Britain. Using carbonised grain and pollen recovered from Iron Age settlements palaeobotanists have demonstrated that new cereals were introduced: emmer wheat gave a higher yield than the original spelt, while diversification into barley, oats and rye extended the growing season and provided some insurance against pests and wet weather (fig. 30). There was extensive regional variation, according to geology and climate. The northern uplands favoured livestock, although there was a lot more arable farming than was once assumed. Scottish coastal communities subsisted on the produce of the sea.

29 *above* Iron farming tools found together at Stantonbury Hill, Somerset. The ploughshare would have been mounted on the wooden frame of the plough. The two reaping hooks are almost identical: tools could be made to a standard pattern. Such basic tools underwent little change until modern machinery and methods were introduced. First century BC or first century AD. L. of ploughshare 287 mm.
30 *below* Reverse of a gold coin depicting an ear of emmer wheat, demonstrating how important its successful cultivation was to the fortunes of the tribe. CAMV is one of the marks stamped on coins of the Trinovantes minted at *Camulodunon*, their main settlement. The coin was found at *Verlamion*, St Albans, Hertfordshire. First century BC.

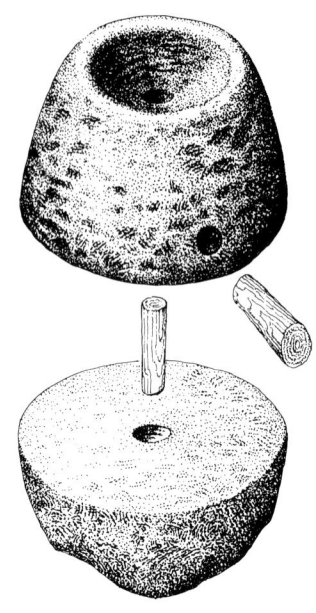

31 Rotary querns to grind corn were first used in Britain in the Iron Age, possibly as early as 400 BC, and continued in use throughout the period of Roman occupation. The bottom stone was set into the ground for stability and so only its upper surface was neatly dressed. The upper stone which rotated on the spindle was completely shaped and finished. Versions with a tall conical upper stone are named 'beehive querns' because the shape is similar to that of old-fashioned beehives. Diam. approximately 260 mm.

All this potentially provided reasonable nutrition although, as we know from our own times, dietary traditions or poverty can lead to unhealthy eating habits. Severe anaemia in some inhabitants of Danebury suggests little fresh fruit or vegetables in their diet. On the other hand, Lindow Man (Lindow II; p. 17) was well nourished. His last meal consisted of baked or griddled unleavened bread made of emmer and spelt wheat mixed with barley. Few plant remains other than cereals survive, but we can assume that edible leaves, flowers, berries and roots often supplemented the diet. Lindow III had consumed a quantity of hazelnuts in his last meal. It is likely that nutritional standards varied widely according to region, social status, and quality of harvest.

Animal bone recovered from settlements – representing pig, cattle, sheep or goats, dogs and horses – provides information about Iron Age husbandry, notably improvements in animal size, and butchery techniques. Milk and dairy products would have been available. Bones of birds and wild species are rare finds, as are fish or shellfish. The use of beeswax in bronze-casting shows honey was available as a sweetener.

Food preparation required simple utensils – a stone quern to grind cereals, containers and a sharp blade to butcher meat. Rotary querns were used at Danebury from the fifth century BC alongside the traditional back-and-forth 'saddle' querns (fig. 31). Suitable grinding stone was brought from 250 km away where necessary. Pots encrusted with sooty residues were probably used for cooking over an open fire. Chemical analysis of these encrustations, still at an early stage, can already distinguish between animal and vegetable fats; more detailed information may be extracted in future.

In the absence of refrigeration, storing the abundance of harvest-time for the lean months of winter was a fundamental problem. Within settlements, carbonised or burnt grain has been found in narrow-mouthed, bell-shaped pits 2–3 m deep (fig. 66). Some at least were probably for bulk storage of grain, for months or more. Rectangular wooden structures supported by four or six posts are also thought to have been granaries or for grain drying. If the 4,500 pits, and rows of 'four-posters' at Danebury were granaries, this hillfort was a gigantic fortified food-store. Large ceramic jars sunk into the ground were perhaps for food storage but they could equally well have been for brewing or some other process.

Foods other than cereals can be preserved by drying, smoking, using salt for dry-curing and pickling in brine or alcohol. Salt has long been a vital ingredient in preserving and there is growing archaeological evidence, in the form of ceramic containers, for its production as a trading commodity.

32 A selection of tools illustrating the wide range made in bone and antler between the eighth and first centuries BC. Bone from domestic animals and antler from hunted species provided abundant and resilient raw materials which in the first millennium BC were widely exploited. They were carved and polished into a variety of pointed and edged tools and equipment needed for crafts like weaving, leather-working and basketry. Antler in particular was used for handles, including sword hilts. L. of handle (bottom row, second left) 96 mm.

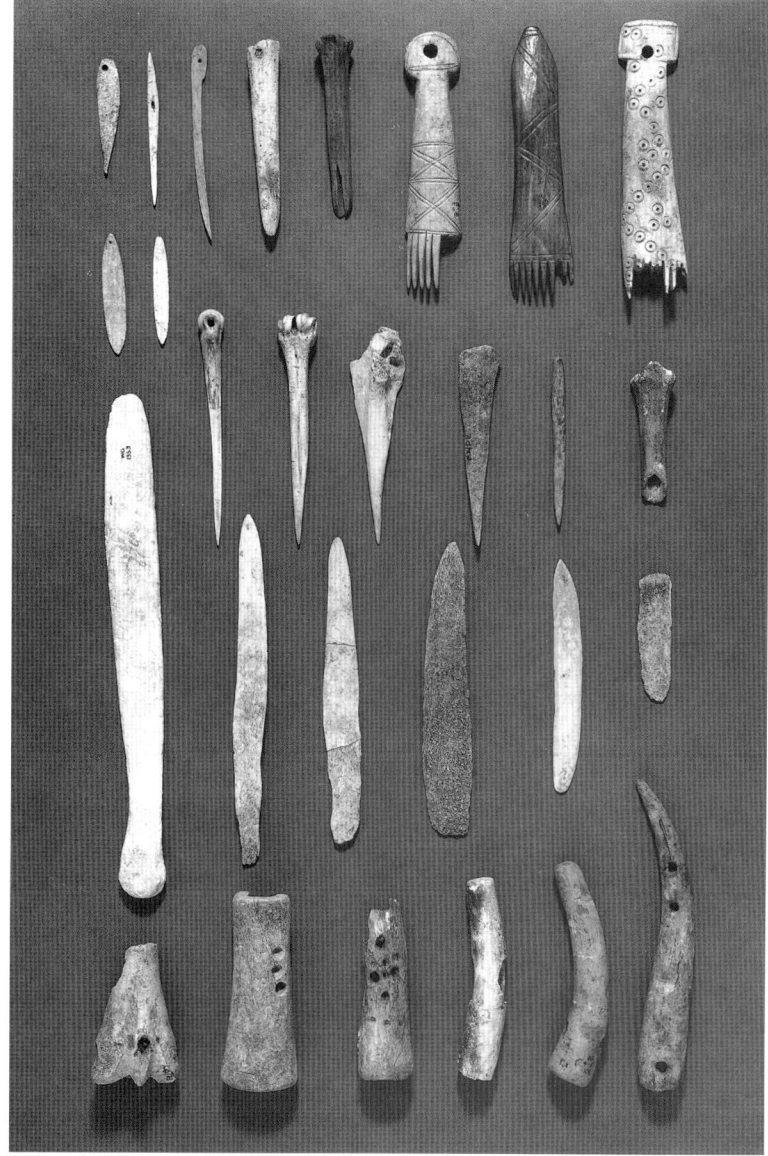

FRUITS OF THE LAND: RAW MATERIALS

Straw for thatch, reed for baskets, wool for textiles, and hides for leatherwork were valuable products of farming which leave scarcely a trace in the archaeological record. This differential loss of perishable organic materials means that their enormous importance in the Iron Age is often seriously underestimated and undervalued today. Horn, antler and bone, by-products of animal husbandry which survive more frequently, were used for ornaments, tools and implement-handles for crafts as diverse as weaving and bronze casting, (figs. 32 and 48).

In bulk, wood was the most important raw material; woodland management was as old as farming. All sizes of timber were required,

33 *left* The lower two surviving steps of an oak 'ladder' with examples of iron axes and an adze of types which were perhaps used to make it. Steps about 100 mm deep and about 430 mm apart were carved in a log about 160 × 160 mm in section and of unknown height. It was found in a waterhole during excavation of a settlement in the Blackwater Valley, at the Tongham Nurseries Site, Surrey, occupied in the second and first centuries BC. It is the only example to be found in Britain and its interpretation remains speculative.

Opposite page

34 *right* The wooden scabbard from Stanwick, Melsonby, North Yorkshire, is a well-preserved example of skilled carpentry using ash, the wood also favoured for stave-built buckets. It was made of twelve individual carved components, glued together and then supported with copper alloy braces and the chape. Found in water-logged conditions in a ditch during excavations of the Stanwick fortifications in 1957, it was rushed to London for immediate conservation treatment. First century AD. L. 730 mm.

35 *far right* One of a pair of wheel impressions excavated from the vehicle burial at Garton Station, East Yorkshire. The wheels had been removed from the vehicle and then leant against the side of the grave. Under normal soil conditions wood disappears without trace, but here the rotting wood left cavities in the hard-packed gravel filling of the grave; then the site flooded, and fine clay was washed into the cavities. The form of the felloe (wooden rim), spokes and nave were all preserved. The wheels have twelve spokes, and mineralised traces on the corroded iron showed that both nave and felloe were made of ash. Diam. approx. 870 mm.

36 *below right* A pedestal jar made of shale, a soft geological deposit of organic origin like jet and coal which was quarried at Kimmeridge, Dorset. Used for vessels and personal ornaments, it became one of the most widely distributed materials in the first millennium BC. This jar is composed of three separate sections, each initially hollowed by hand and then finished on a lathe to produce accurate overlapped joints and decorative raised cordons. The same techniques could have been used with wood: there is evidence that lathe-turned wood vessels were made in Britain before wheel-thrown pots. This is one of a matching pair buried with a cremation in the early first century at Old Warden, Bedfordshire. Only the top section survives; the base was restored following the second example. Restored H. 350 mm.

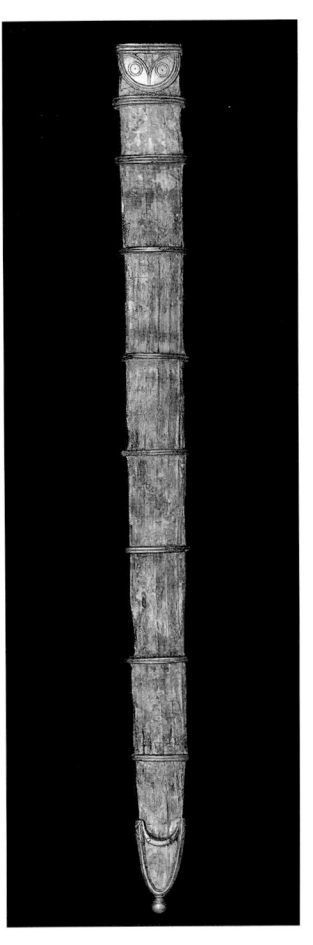

from mature trees, especially oak for building (fig. 33), to sapling wood for fencing and fuel, particularly to make charcoal for smelting.

Wood was vital for basic tools like ploughs, and for spear-shafts and shields. Wood-workers selected particular species of timber for specific functions. Vehicles required great carpentry skills – three different types of wood were used for a wheel found at Holme Pierpoint, Nottinghamshire. Finds from water-logged settlements at Glastonbury and Meare, Somerset (300–50 BC) demonstrate the varied uses of wood. Besides stave-built, hand-carved and bent-wood containers there are lathe-turned vessels, showing that the techniques for producing standardised wooden components on a large scale were introduced before the kick-wheel was adopted in pot-making (fig. 36).

Wool is the only textile fibre identified in Britain during the first millennium BC, although flax and even badger-hair were processed in continental Europe. Nothing remains of dyeing processes although it can be supposed that urine was used as a mordant to fix dyes derived

37 A selection of fired clay spindle whorls and loom-weights, combs, shuttles and needles of bone and antler used in the first millennium BC. Generally it is only the equipment in durable materials which survives as evidence for the important crafts of spinning, weaving and sewing. Practicalities dictate that, while spinning and braid-weaving could be mobile occupations suitable for long hours tending herds at seasonal pastures, handloom weaving was static and best suited to permanent settlements. H. of the triangular loomweight 136 mm.

from plants and coloured earths. Surviving equipment, and imprints of textiles reveal use of warp-weighted looms for wide cloth, and tablet weaving for narrow braids (fig. 37). Yarn spun in opposite directions, twill-weaving and embroidery produce a wide variety of stripes, checks and diamond-shaped motifs while braids, fringes, tassels and thread-work can add more ornament and colour.

Cloth-production and garment-making are often assumed to have been women's tasks; spindle-whorls have indeed been found in female burials at Kirkburn and Arras (East Yorkshire), but weaving tools are found only in settlements. While spindle whorls are scattered throughout the Glastonbury lake village, loomweights are concentrated in three huts, perhaps implying that three families specialised in cloth production.

Pot sherds are the most numerous artefact found on any permanent Iron Age settlement, although they are less plentiful on sites in the North and West, due variously to lower levels of pottery usage, poorer raw materials leading to less durable pots, or more chemically destructive soils.

Domestically, they were used for storing, preparing, cooking and eating food, and perhaps for transporting it. During exchange they could be used to measure foodstuffs like cereals and nuts. There is evidence for the increasing standardisation of size and shape which this would require. Finely finished examples could have been given as gifts or tribute. In some regions and periods pots were important in ritual and were deposited in burials and other offerings.

Perhaps more than any other craft, pottery-making presented a widely variable degree of added value. Raw materials were easily obtained, and little specialist skill was needed to produce a usable pot. The input of time and effort could be geared to requirements of the consumer, anything from the most basic, plain pot to highly finished special offerings. Moreover the scale of production was easily varied from a few vessels for immediate domestic needs to a surplus for exchange when necessary.

The raw materials were water, fuel and clay mixed with a 'temper' like crushed flint, sand or 'grog' (crushed pottery) which reduced shrinkage and cracking on drying, and allowed water in the fabric to escape when the pots were fired. Until the first century BC pots were hand-made by coil- or slab-shaping, with the joins carefully smoothed over. Fired under a bonfire on the ground or in a shallow pit, the pot's colour depended on the chemistry of the clay and the firing conditions. If the fuel was dry, the smoke light in colour and oxygen present, the result was orange or red oxidised pots. When the fuel was damp, the smoke was black and sooty and so dark grey or black pots were produced.

Archaeologists categorise pots by finish and presumed function into coarse (kitchen) and fine (table) wares. The surfaces of coarse-wares were simply smoothed-off using the fingers, producing a matt finish when fired. Finewares were burnished smooth so that a glossy finish resulted. A special range of glossy red finewares was popular in southern Britain. Iron-rich clay which turned red on firing with oxygen and resisted the blackening effects of smoke was applied to the outer surface of a limited range of bowls and jars. By the end of the second century BC regional styles of decoration using burnished, incised and excised patterns had emerged.

The kick-wheel, or fast-wheel, was widely used around the Mediterranean by 1200 BC. It facilitated the large-scale production of standardised vessels and its widespread adoption in pot-making

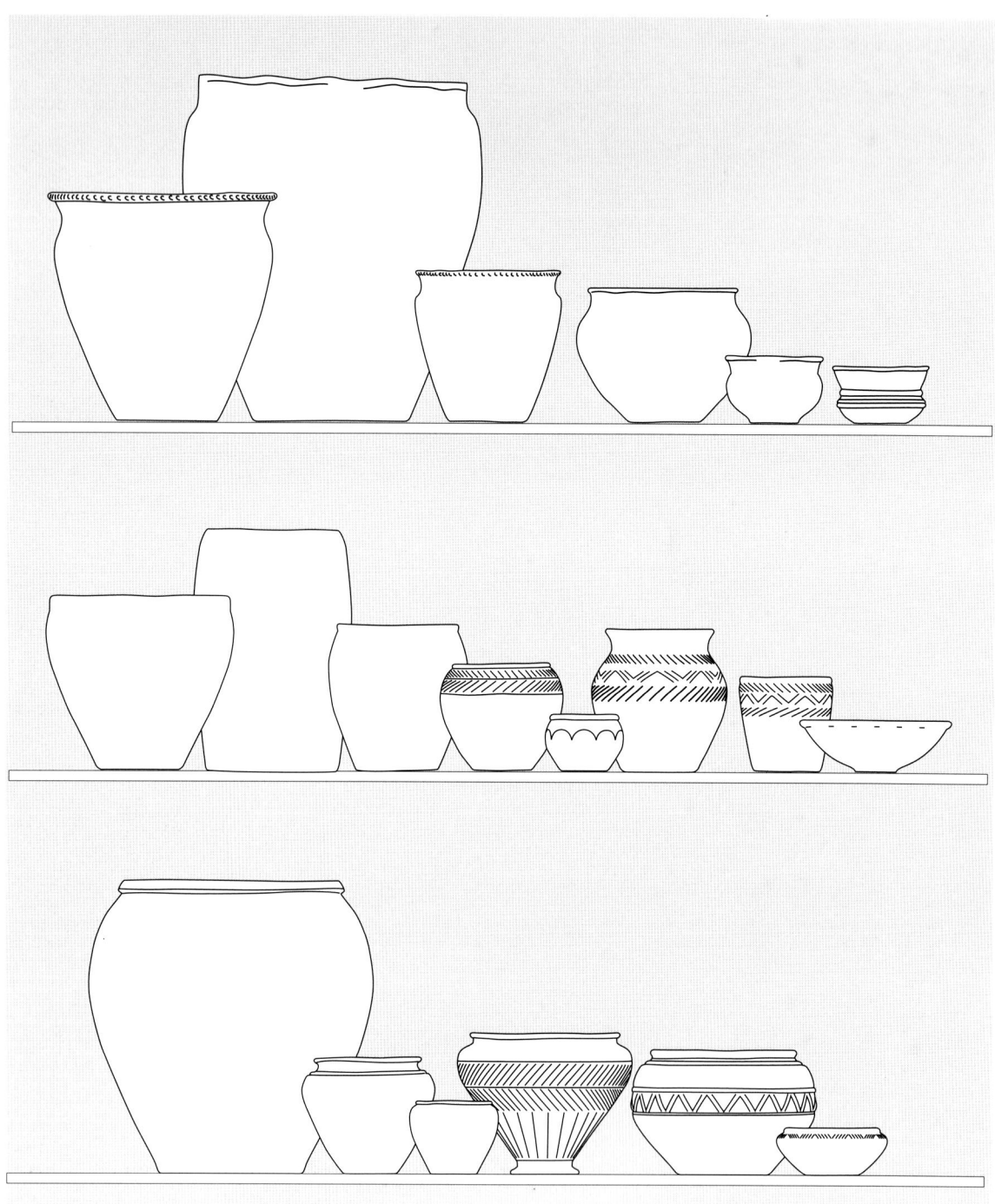

38 *above* The changing shape of handmade pots in southern Britain 450 to 50 BC. Simple shapeless forms with plain or textured surfaces were gradually replaced by more definite shapes with incised, stamped and burnished decoration.

39 *opposite page* The changing shape of wheel-thrown pots in eastern Britain between 80 BC and AD 50. Wheel-throwing favoured the production of sinuous shapes with horizontal grooves and raised cordons. While Italian wine was imported from the late second century BC,

the fine table wares used for serving and consuming food and drink according to Gaulish manners were not imported until later, in the late first century BC. The specialised shapes of flagons, platters and drinking-cups were then immediately copied by British potters.

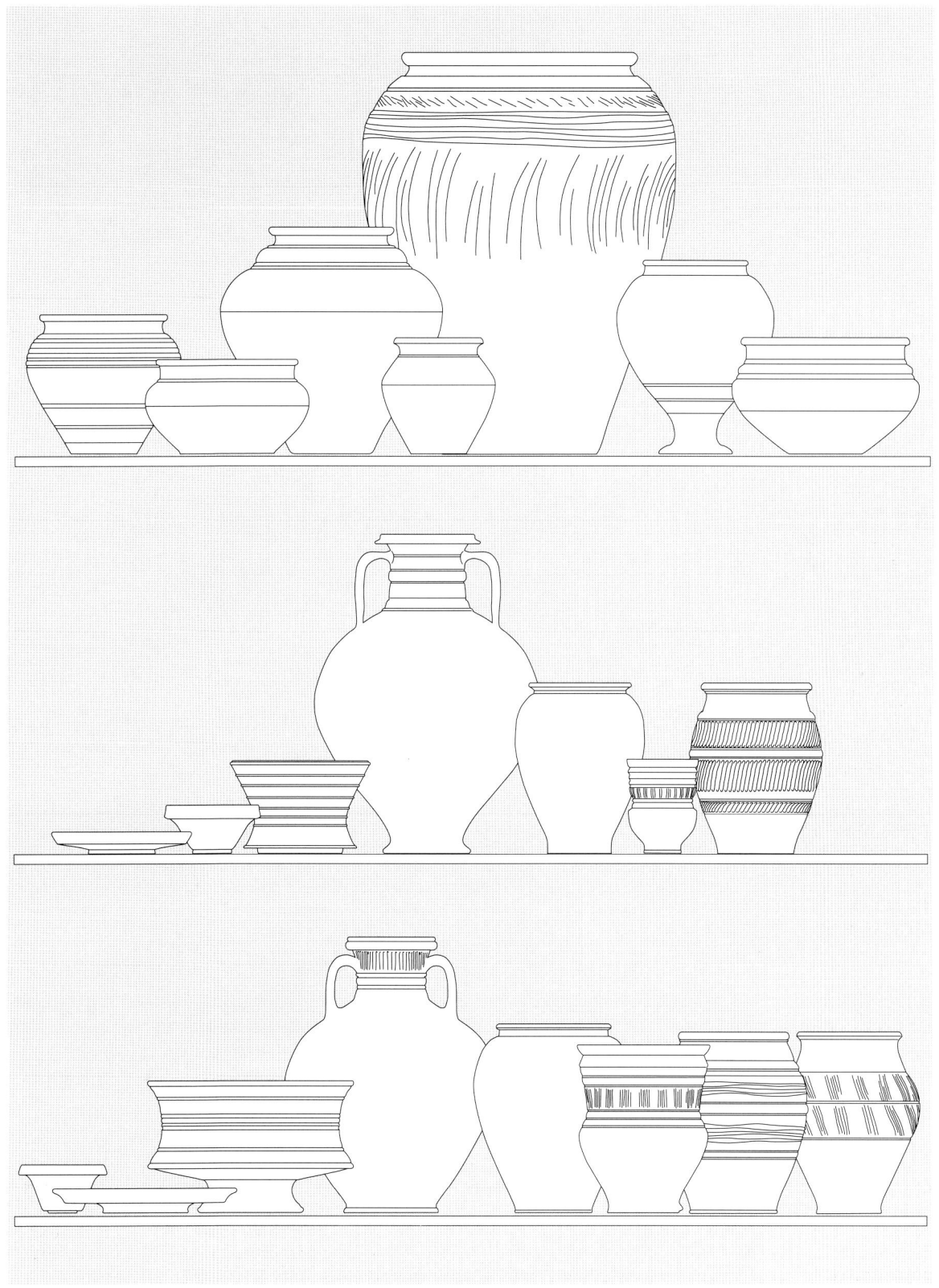

40 Decorated pots dating to the first century BC from Little Woodbury, Wiltshire, Glastonbury, Somerset, Margate, Kent, and Mucking, Essex. During the first millennium the majority of British artefacts were not decorated; even pots which could have been easily patterned with burnished or incised lines before firing were left plain. By the beginning of the first century BC potters in different areas accepted the potential of pottery for ornament and display and, using specialised techniques, evolved distinctive regional styles of decoration. H. of pot on extreme left 100 mm.

implies a demand for such products and a market network for their distribution. Until both factors were in place there was no reason to change from hand-shaping techniques. Although some wheel-thrown vessels were made in Europe north of the Alps in the fifth century BC, widespread production did not occur until the third century and the technique was not introduced to southern Britain until the beginning of the first century BC.

Despite adoption of wheel-throwing techniques and large-scale output, vessels continued to be fired in bonfires and hence were still made in heavily tempered fabrics, limited to drab earth colours. Specially constructed pottery kilns, allowing finer, more colourful fabrics, were not introduced until Roman times.

Throughout the first millennium BC vessel-shapes evolved, although basic techniques remained the same. Vessels with a sharply angled shoulder gave way to 'shapeless' types. Initially these vessels were finished with a tall conical rim, later replaced by a narrow bead-shaped rim or even no rim at all. Subsequently pots with s-shaped profiles were developed. Wheel-throwing favoured the production of curvaceous shapes enhanced by adding horizontal raised cordons and incised grooves. In the first century BC the resulting southern Britain vessels were very like those made in western Gaul. The potters would have been equally at home on either side of the Channel.

The earliest wheel-thrown pots were imported from Italy and Gaul. They were vessels for eating, and particularly for drinking imported wine in the approved Roman manner. Local potters quickly adopted the shapes – shallow platters, foot-ring cups, flasks and han-dled flagons – but continued to produce them in traditional grog-tempered fabrics. Examples of these local copies occur more commonly in burials than in contemporary settlements suggesting that the impetus for their adoption was religious, particularly for funerary banquets and perhaps other ceremonial feasting.

METALWORKING

By 500 BC iron had replaced bronze as the metal to make essential edged tools and weapons throughout continental Europe. There were important differences between iron and bronze production. Iron could not be cast like bronze because temperatures achieved in furnaces were too low to melt iron. When iron ore was smelted a spongy mixture of metal droplets and impurities collected at the bottom of the furnace and this 'bloom' had to be further refined by repeated heating and hammering to remove impurities. Since the wrought iron produced in this way was not inherently superior to bronze in its functional characteristics, two factors may have promoted change. Iron ore deposits are much more widely available and accessible than those of the copper, tin and lead used in bronzes. And despite smelting problems, wrought iron can be fabricated into artefacts in ways that bronze cannot. Its strength and durability are improved by repeated heating, cooling, bending, twisting and hammering.

Workable deposits of iron ore occur widely in Britain. Since most of the ore consists of unwanted impurities, initial smelting presumably took place at the quarry to reduce bulk before transportation. Archaeological evidence for iron-working in the early Iron Age is sparse compared to that for the Roman and later periods. None of the processes from the first roasting of the ore to the final honing of a sword demanded large permanent installations.

Scarcely a settlement of Iron Age date has not produced slag, suggesting that ironworking, like potting, was a common element of everyday life. Caesar reported that Britons used iron bars of fixed weight as currency – hence 'currency bars' (fig. 87). It is now assumed that such ingots of standard quality were traded into areas without sources of good iron ore.

Iron tools were made to standard patterns and sizes for the farmer, smith, woodsman and carpenter (figs. 29 and 41). Occasionally shears, cutting-wheels or tracers, hammers and engraving tools are found,

41 A selection of tools typical of the blacksmith's forge in the Late Iron Age and Roman periods, found together at Waltham Abbey, Essex. The smith used the tongs to hold the heated iron on the anvil so that it could be hammered into shape. The file was used for cold-shaping and finishing. Both tools and forging techniques changed little from the pre-Roman Iron Age until the early years of the present century. L. of file 232 mm.

42 A selection of edged tools forged in iron. Knives had been made since the Bronze Age, but shears were a later innovation more suited to the tensile properties of iron. By the first century BC iron shears were made in a range of sizes: the smallest here would have been for personal use, while the largest pair could have been for pruning or sheep-shearing. The revolving disc was another new tool which could be used to measure distance or with a sharpened edge could be used as a cutter. L. of small shears 100 mm.

but few can be attributed to a specific craft (fig. 42). Iron-tipped spears and javelins were the main weapon for hunting and war. Iron tools occasionally appear as grave goods. A blacksmith, buried with a sword to denote his status, was found at Kirkburn, East Yorkshire, while at Whitcombe, Dorset, another swordsman was equipped with a hammer and bow-drill.

CRAFTS OF DISPLAY

Metals were never simply used for tools and weapons. Their bright, shining finish was exploited for ornament. Since many ores were found in few places, long-distance exchange developed. Control of extraction and distribution meant wealth and power for an individual or community. A conspicuous display of ornament demonstrated access to, and control of, precious resources denied to the majority.

Deprived of demand for tools by the change from bronze to iron, bronzeworkers concentrated on ornamental products. Bronze Age smiths had already developed great skills in casting and sheet-metal work in gold and copper alloys; after 400 BC they concentrated on enhancing the aesthetic aspects of bronze. New decorative motifs were developed and contrasting colour was applied in the form of other metals, pink and white coral and inlays of coloured glass, particularly red.

Bronze mirrors provided an ideal medium for demonstrating both casting and engraving skills of the highest order (figs. 43 and 44).

43 *below right* The decorated back of a bronze mirror found at Aston, Hertfordshire. The motif can be interpreted as an abstract or hidden face. While they were clearly symbols of high status because of the craftsmanship they demonstrate, mirrors have properties which make them objects of particular mystery in many cultures. Any image has right and left transposed, while the viewer can see forwards and backwards at the same time. Late first century BC. Diam. 194 mm.

44 *far right* An enlarged detail showing the technique used to engrave the basket weave texture which formed the pattern on the back of the Aston Mirror. There is no outline to the design and no guidelines have been found; since the overall design is symmetrical and reasonably accurate it suggests that a drawn out pattern remained in place over the area to be decorated throughout the operation. The graver had a sharp edge which produced unusually fine lines. Lines were incised in uneven blocks, orientated at right angles to produce the basket-weave effect where the design is sufficiently wide, but in one direction, at an angle, where it is narrow.

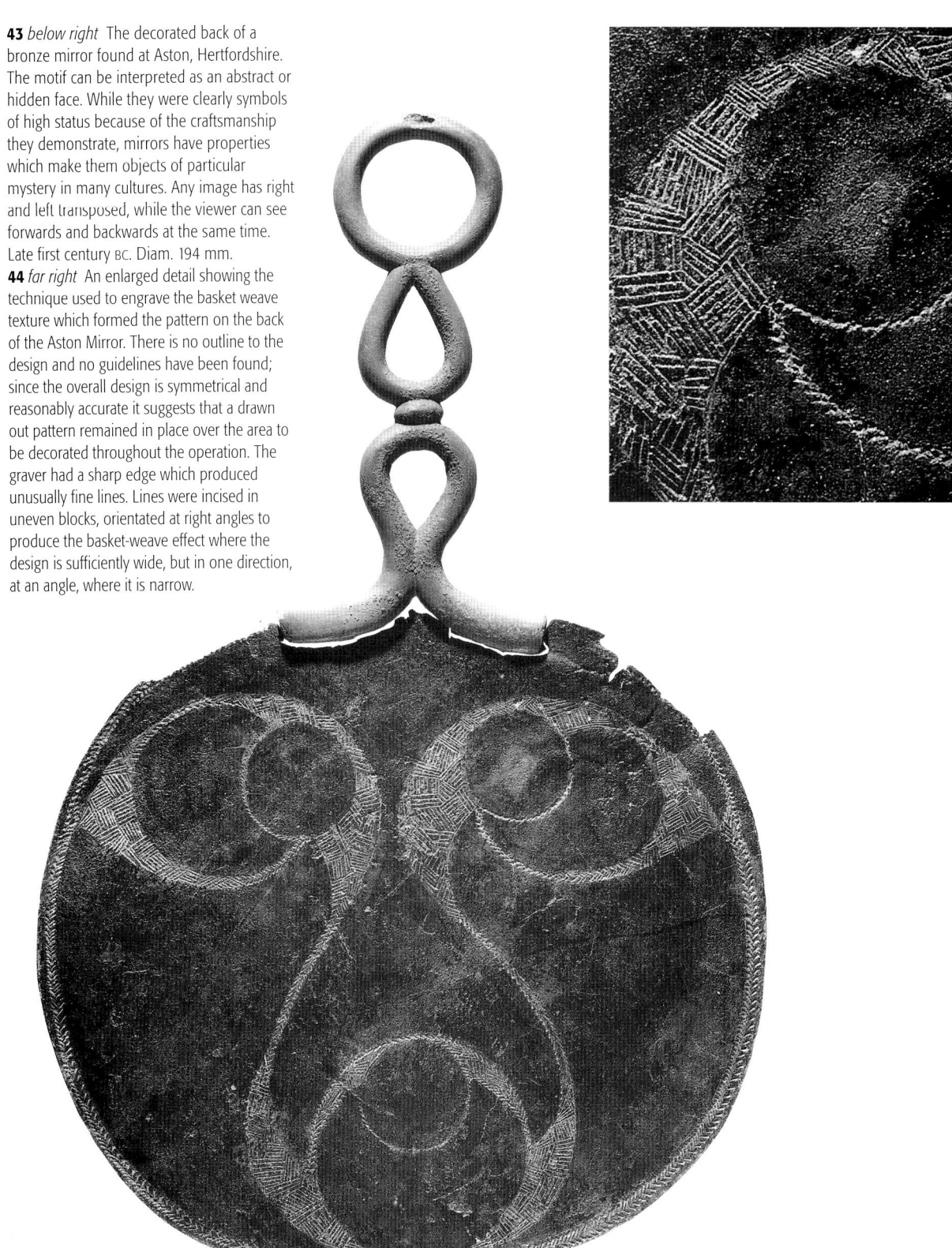

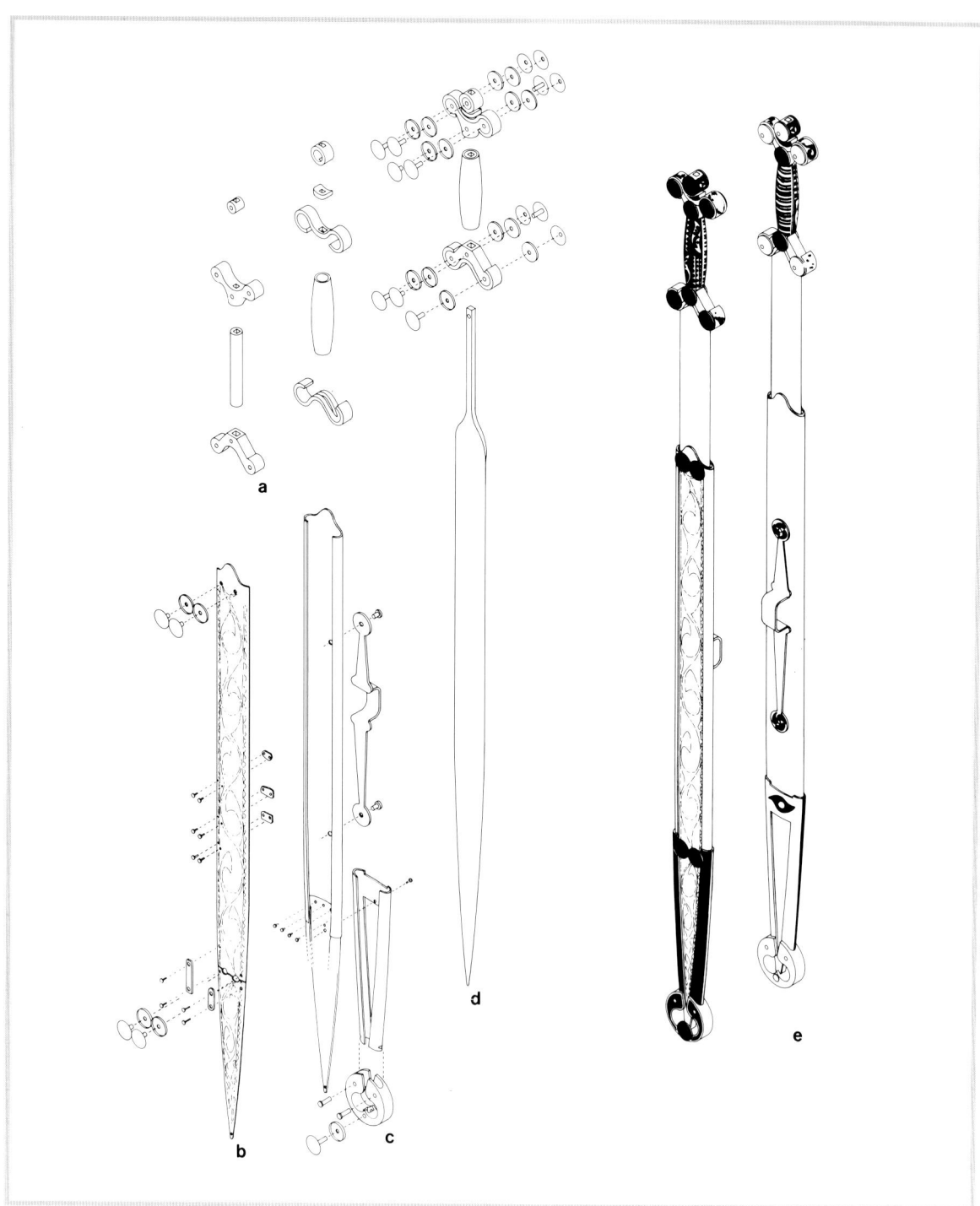

45 Assembling the components of a sword and matching scabbard found in an inhumation grave in the Kirkburn Cemetery, East Yorkshire. The scabbard's front plate is bronze but the back plate, chape and sword hilt are of iron, so combining the contrasting colours of silvery grey iron and golden bronze. More colour was provided by inlaid opaque red glass and applied studs decorating the hilt and scabbard. Made early in the third century BC, this sword and scabbard show the earliest examples of inlaid opaque red glass ornament yet found in Britain. L. of scabbard 592 mm.

Bronze shields were fabricated from numerous separate sheet and cast components and decorated with combinations of repoussé, chased and engraved motifs. Nine separate components make up the Chertsey shield while the Battersea shield required over ninety (figs. 67 and 12). Vessels were raised from a single sheet or assembled from several (fig. 47).

A sword was the attribute of a prominent warrior. Between the sixth and first centuries BC the size, shape and proportions of the blade changed markedly, perhaps reflecting new fighting techniques (fig. 7). Time and effort were expended on the sword-hilt and scabbard. Iron, bronze, wood, leather, antler, horn, coral and red glass were employed to spectacular effect while scabbard front-plates of iron or bronze sported flowing engraved patterns (fig. 45).

Matching sets of bronze harness fittings for a two-horse vehicle comprising bits, terrets, strap unions and linch-pins were especially popular. Charioteers in the army raised by Cassivellaunus to oppose Caesar needed 4,000 sets, that is at least 44,000 individual items.

46 *below* An iron sword stamped twice with a maker's mark depicting a horse motif similar to those found on British coins: the impressions are inlaid with brass. Stamps may indicate the use of special metal or production by a swordsmith of high repute. This example, found in the Thames at Syon Reach, Isleworth, Middlesex, is the only inlaid sword to have been recognised in Britain. Second or first century BC. W. 44 mm.

47 *above* Two bronze vessels illustrating different sheet metal techniques. The bowl found at Lochar Moss, Aberdeenshire, was raised and shaped in a single piece without seams. In contrast, the cauldron found in a ditch at Spettisbury Rings, Dorset, is made up of three different components with overlapped seams secured with dome-headed rivets. An iron hoop strengthened the rim edge and there are scars on the outside where a pair of iron ring handles used for suspending the cauldron had been attached. A similar but larger cauldron was found in the 'chieftain burial' at Baldock, Hertfordshire (fig. 90). Diam. of cauldron rim 260 mm.

48 *above* Some of the raw materials, bone modelling tools, fired clay crucibles and moulds used to cast at least fifty sets of horse-harness in the Late Iron Age at Gussage-All-Saints, Dorset. Gussage was a small settlement of no more than two houses, yet for one short period in the first century BC it was a hive of activity, making prestige cast bronzes. Then all products were removed from the site and all debris was cleared up and buried.

The cake of raw opaque red glass was found in London and the triangular metal ingots at Essendon, Hertfordshire. L. of bone tool (bottom left) 80 mm.

49 *opposite page* A selection of horse-harness to illustrate the colourful effects of inlaying opaque red glass into cast bronzes. Prepared cakes of red glass like that in fig. 48 were imported. Blue, yellow and white were used more sparingly. First and second century AD. L. of linchpin 80 mm.

'Lost wax' technique was used to cast up to nine inter-linked components of a bridle-bit. Mould-debris from bronze-casting is sufficiently common to suggest production was by itinerant specialists (fig. 48).

Coral and glass added permanent bright colour to metal objects. Application of decorative studs and coloured inlay to metal objects was never limited to Britain, but in the first century AD metal-workers and enamellers achieved a quality unsurpassed within or on the fringes of the Roman empire. Weapons and harness fittings were elaborately embellished with scrolls or geometric patterns in opaque red, blue or yellow enamel, pieces now amongst the most admired items of early British art (fig. 49).

The first sight of a vehicle must have been stunning, its harness glistening with trappings of golden metal inlaid with sealing-wax red. The intensity and quality of the red is uncommon in nature – it is most typical of transient berries and fruits in autumn. Even scarlet arterial blood fades in seconds. Natural dyes could not produce such intensity in textiles. Red and pink coral can be bright, but red glass was the one material which could be worked to produce an expanse of seamless, permanent, intense and rare colour.

50 *above* A framed stud from the Battersea shield (damaged) shows how these studs were made. Softened red glass was pushed into the cast bronze frame from the back then the front surface was polished. Twenty-seven studs of this type in four different sizes were used in groups to ornament specific sections of the shield. The whole shield can be seen in fig. 12. Third century BC. Diam. 31 mm.

51 *right* A non-identical pair of discs ornamented with studs to resemble preserved holly or rowan berries found in a warrior burial at Bugthorpe, North Yorkshire. Each is composed of nine unframed studs secured with iron rivets to a shaped bronze plate. The highly domed shape was made by covering a ceramic core with a thin skin of opaque red glass, thus producing the maximum effect using the minimum of rare glass. Second century BC. Diam. 60 mm.

The studs on the Battersea shield may represent drops of blood, but the high relief studs grouped as a roundel and secured with dark rivets on the Bugthorpe discs are surely a permanent display of holly or rowan berries (figs. 50 and 51). Similarly, it can be argued that small white coral studs which adorn brooches in particular are everlasting mistletoe berries, reminders of that most sacred of evergreens which could only be gathered, at least according to Pliny, with a golden sickle.

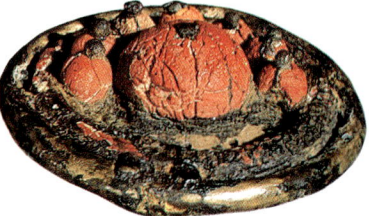

GOLD

Gold is a heavy and scarce resource. Smiths quickly learnt to produce the maximum visible surface area for the minimum weight of metal through gilding or alloying with silver or base metals. Gold is also soft and can be worked cold so, where practicable, items were assembled from components of sheet, wire and granules soldered together rather than cast in one piece.

Cassius Dio described Boudica as wearing a 'gold necklet' symbolising religious and political authority, while Strabo listed gold as a British export. Until 1948 finds other than coins did not suggest gold was abundant in Iron Age Britain, since there were just ten torcs made of twisted bar or wire. Discoveries since 1948 near to previous findspots in the English Midlands and more particularly in East Anglia have radically changed the picture and almost one hundred intact or virtually complete torcs are now known. That the pattern can be so drastically altered by a few finds shows how tenuous our knowledge still remains of many aspects of the Iron Age.

There is over 30 kg of bullion in the Snettisham Hoards – sufficient to pay a mercenary army of perhaps 6,000 men for a year or a Roman legion for five years. There is no convincing evidence yet of Iron Age gold or silver mining on the British mainland despite the evidence of Roman extraction of precious metals in Wales and the South-West, so where did such an amount of precious metal originate? Ireland is often claimed as a source of alluvial gold. Gold coins were used to pay mercenaries and this could be a significant import route assuming that Britons served in large numbers, as Gauls did in the armies of the Greek kingdoms. The slave trade may also have contributed along with ransom, tribute, bribery or munificent gifts and dowries.

Evidence for working in precious metals is as thin as that for iron-

and bronze-working. Ingots and scrap were found at Snettisham, Norfolk, but no furnace debris, crucibles or tools (fig. 53). Fragments of fired clay moulds used in the production of metal pellets for stamping into coins occur in many important Late Iron Age settlements.

CONTINENTAL CONNECTIONS

Continental ideas, fashions, and technologies were imported to Britain, but selectively. The pattern is primarily one of strong local traditions, into which foreign ideas were incorporated and reinterpreted, if they were not rejected. In certain areas, evidence such as pottery is consistent with localised immigration; but the differences from the Continent remain at least as important as the similarities. There were varied and often intimate contacts, but not wholesale migrations, in the South, while more conservative patterns prevailed in the North.

52 The terminal of the torc found at Sedgeford, Norfolk. The colour, shape and technique typify British gold-work of the Late Iron Age.

The rather pale gold colour is due to the addition of a high proportion of silver. The neck-ring was made from over 25 m of 2 mm gauge handmade wire cut into forty-eight lengths which were twisted together in three separate operations. Initially the forty-eight wires were tightly twisted in pairs into strands, then groups of three strands were twisted in the opposite direction and finally the resulting eight components were coiled around a former to make a hollow tube about 30 mm in diameter. A hollow loop terminal, ornamented in relief, was added at each end. Many of the gold and silver alloy torcs found in Britain conform to this basic pattern, although they differ in the gauge and number of wires, and the number and direction of twists used. Twisted wire gave the neck-ring flexibility. About 70 BC. Surviving L. 184 mm.

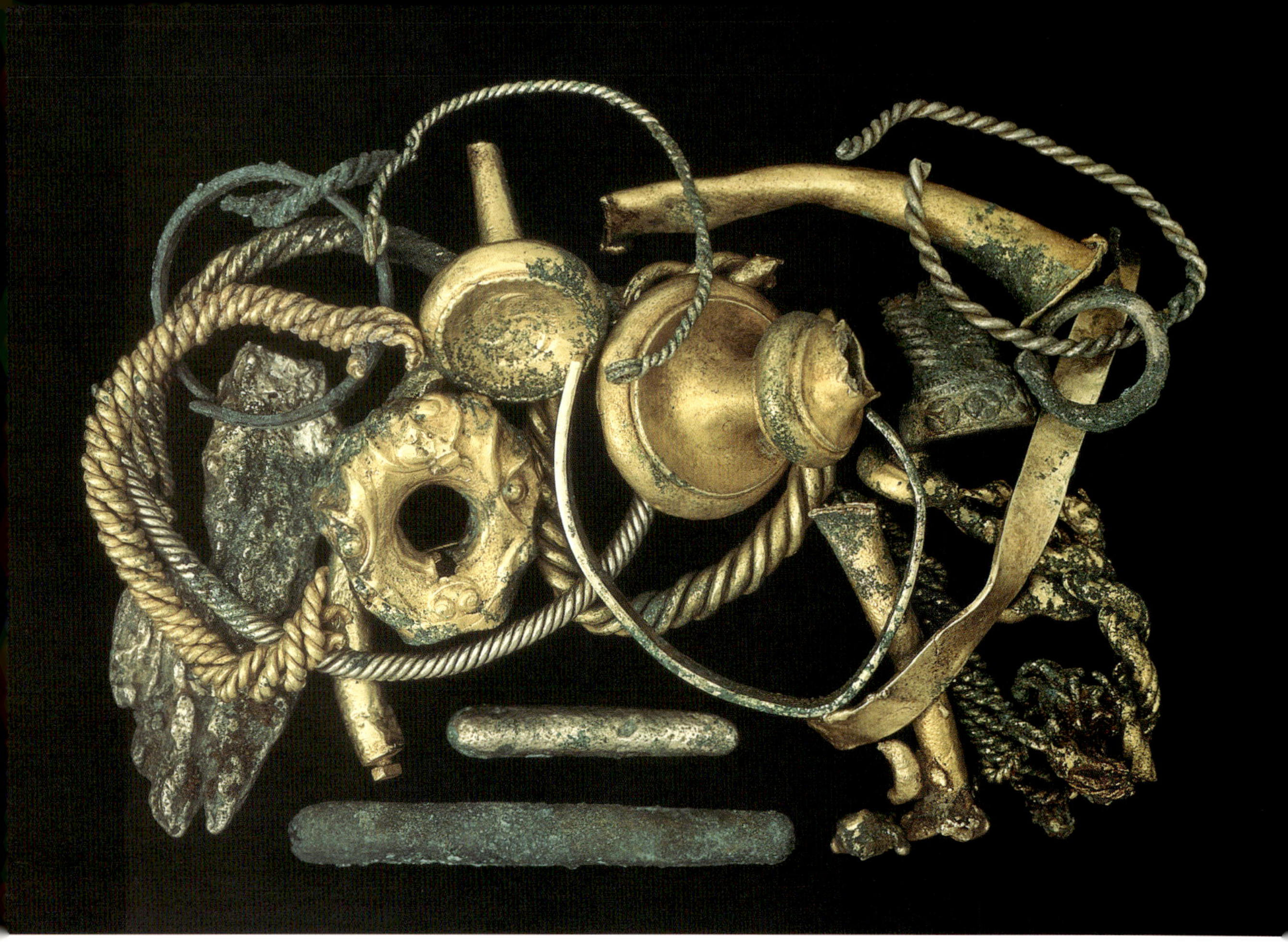

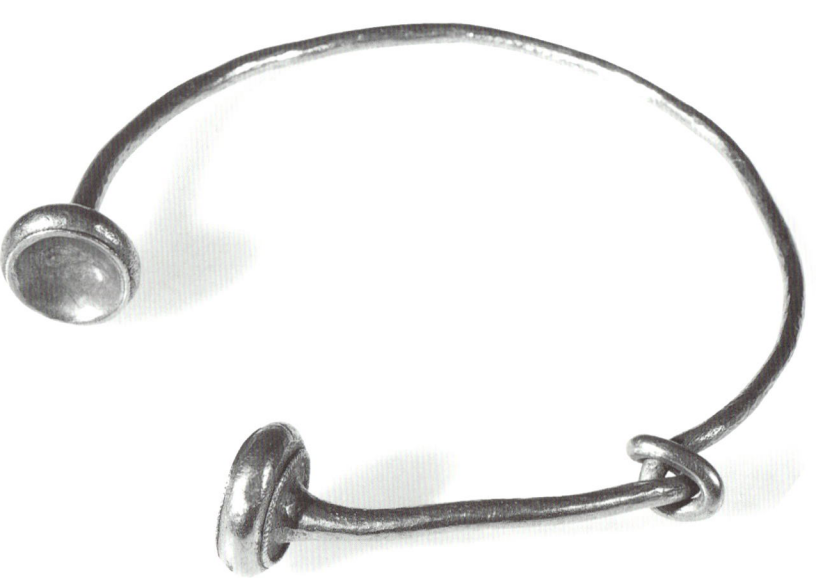

54 A hollow torc with buffer terminals: the neck-ring was shortened by a knot. It was published as being in the collection of the British Museum in 1848 but even then was without provenance. The form, with its narrow tubular neck-ring and markedly flared terminals, relates more closely to torcs produced in continental Europe than the insular British type with its twisted wire neck-ring. Third century BC. Diam. 151 mm.

53 *opposite page, top* A selection of cast ingots, semi-finished ingot rings and fragmented ornaments which comprise the metalworkers' hoard (Hoard F) found at Snettisham, Norfolk. Hoard F is a typical 'founder's hoard' of scrap metal apparently collected for re-cycling which was buried in a single vessel of sheet bronze now surviving only in small fragments. Many of the 500 separate items illustrate stylistic or technical features not hitherto recognised in Britain and demonstrate a more varied range of skills than was suggested by existing finds. Twelve buffer terminals for plain hollow torcs are of a type known previously only from a single example with no provenance (see fig. 54). It includes gold, silver, bronze and tin separately and variously alloyed, as well as several examples of gilded silver and bronze wire, and even one where gold has been superimposed on gilt bronze wire. The hoard was buried early in the first century BC.

This page
55 *top* A squashed buffer terminal from a hollow gold torc found in Hoard F, Snettisham, Norfolk. The relief ornament combines the techniques of chasing and engraving to produce the most complex curvilinear design yet found on a gold torc in Britain. It demonstrates that the skills of gold-workers were not inferior to those of bronze-smiths. Surviving L. 130 mm.

56 *bottom* Gold torcs buried together in the early first century BC at Ipswich, Suffolk. Five similar torcs were each made of two twisted solid gold bars. The relief decoration on the terminals divides into two (not quite identical) pairs. The torc with plain terminals was made of faceted bars which produces a particularly pleasing effect. The sixth and odd torc was made from two pairs of narrower gauge gold wire twisted together in two operations. Diam. of wire torc 188 mm.

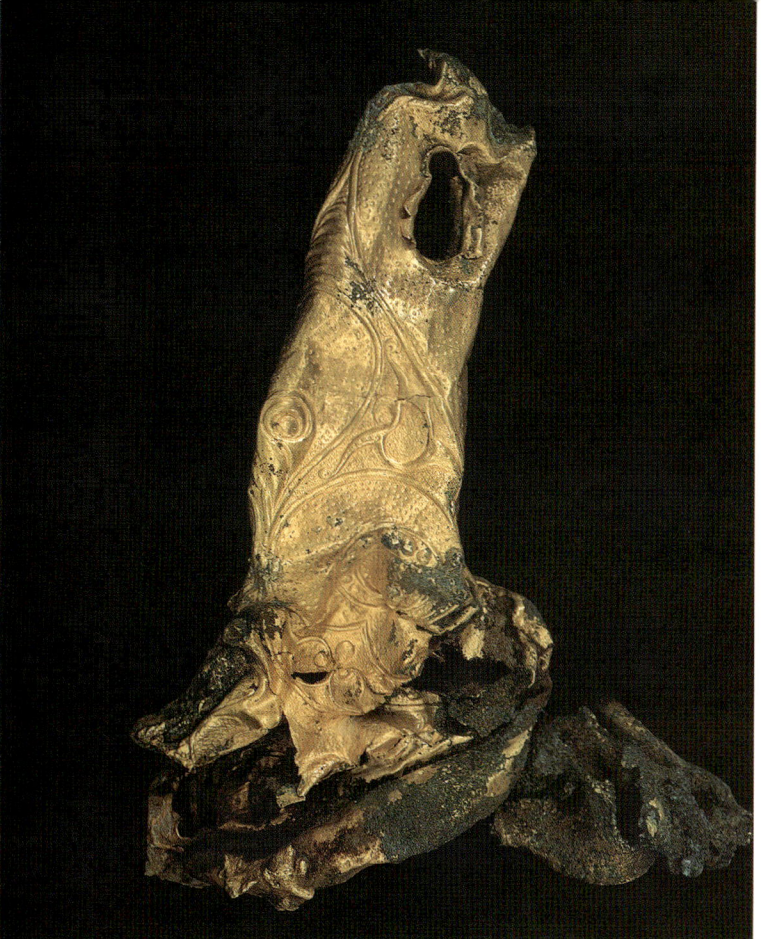

4 Settlements and societies

Opposite page

57 *top* A watercolour reconstruction of the Early Iron Age enclosed settlement of Staple Howe, Yorkshire, painted by Alan Sorrel in the 1960s. On a chalk hillock overlooking the Vale of Pickering, at the edge of the Yorkshire Wolds, Staple Howe was home in the seventh century BC to a small farming community keeping cattle, sheep and pigs. Carbonised wheat was also found. The square structure of massive posts in the centre is interpreted as a granary.

58 *bottom* The Glastonbury 'lake village' in the Somerset Levels, as envisaged by Amédée Forestier, a pioneer of archaeological reconstruction illustration, in 1911. Some of the detail is now known to be incorrect or anachronistic, but it still gives a good atmospheric general impression of what the village probably looked like. The excavation of the site between 1892 and 1917 by Arthur Bulleid and Harold St George Gray is one of the classics of British archaeology. More accurately described as a swamp-village, the site has been recently reappraised and it is now suggested that it was occupied from perhaps 250 BC to around 50 BC when it was abandoned, perhaps due to environmental changes.

Archaeology has much to tell about the physical nature of the Iron Age Britons, and the basic practices of their lives. What can it say about how these people shaped their world and understood their place in it, at the personal level of family life, and at the level of larger groupings leading up to the tribes or kingdoms described by Caesar?

The Classical sources depict the Britons of the Late Iron Age as divided into many separate *civitates* (*civitas* means 'city-state' or more generally 'polity', an organised society; in the context of Britain usually translated as 'tribe'). It may be tempting to extrapolate backwards from the Greco-Roman sources, and the most visually striking archaeological evidence, to assume that Iron Age Britain was dominated by warrior nobles and hillforts. However, archaeology lets us look at the centuries, regions, and the many aspects of life beyond the limited scope of the texts, which only really tell us about some facets of the Late Iron Age South. The picture which then appears is complex and surprising.

Archaeological clues to the social order of past cultures derive from a number of sources, not least cemeteries but, as we have seen, these are lacking for most of the British Iron Age. The way people treat the dead is in any case a special set of circumstances and rites. We also want to know about the living, their homes, and the land on which they spent their days. For late prehistoric Britain, archaeology compensates for the dearth of cemetery evidence with a remarkable record of land-use and settlement, from farms and field-systems to fortifications.

EVOLVING IDEAS

Early Classics-educated archaeologists were predisposed to focus on military aspects of the Iron Age. Prominent finds of arms, and the massive presence of hillforts like Maiden Castle, Dorset, seemed to confirm the primacy of war (figs. 12, 13). Yet finds of weapons are actually rare for much of the earlier Iron Age, and many hilly areas never developed hillforts. There are also many other classes of monument in Britain which reveal a great diversity of settlement forms, some defended, many not (figs. 57 and 58). In the rocky North and West, where stone was more abundant than wood, forms are to be seen as varied as the brochs of Atlantic Scotland (fig. 59), the stone-walled

59 The broch of Dun Telve, in Gleann Beag, near Glenelg in the Western Highlands of Scotland. The surviving portion of the tower-like structure reveals chambers within the wall. Although built without mortar, the broch's circular shape and tapering profile made for strength and stability. Brochs are a feature of Northern Scotland and the Isles from the later Iron Age.

farmsteads of the Pennines and the cliff-castles, rounds and 'fogous' (underground chambers) of Cornwall. Focusing on arms and hillforts gives a 'top-down' view of *some* British societies. The newer archaeology of settlement and land use produces very different views of Iron Age communities, literally and figuratively from the ground up.

Since World War II excavation and survey have revealed hidden Iron Age landscapes, revolutionising our picture even of the supposedly hillfort-dominated South. In some areas apparently complete patterns of settlement and land division have been recovered, allowing us to make inferences about the nature of the societies that created them.

SMALL, DIVERSE SOCIETIES

Archaeology suggests that most communities were organised on a very small, local level, with limited outside contacts. Those living a few miles away might be considered alien. There was certainly inter-action between neighbouring groups, for example through exchange of marriage partners and of goods not available locally (metals, salt), perhaps at periodic religious festivals and fairs. Intermarriage will have provided links of kinship and common descent which could form the basis of larger groupings. And where there was contact and co-operation, there will also have been conflict.

Geology, climate and ecology provided resources for human com-munities to exploit. But they also placed limits on the productivity possible with the domestic animal breeds, crop varieties, tools and techniques available. The diversity of landscapes in Britain and the difficulties and opportunities of communication between them, constrained and channelled inter-communal contacts. This encour-aged a mosaic of many social groupings with diverse ways of life, social organisations and settlement patterns. Atlantic communities, although hemmed in by wet, hilly land with poor soil, enjoyed good sea communications and the productivity of the ocean. The latter was denied to inlanders of the Upper Thames Valley who, in con-trast, had richer soils to exploit. Such land gave the South and East the potential to support larger populations, and more elaborate social hierarchies, than the upland regions.

As Barry Cunliffe and others have observed, as late as, say, 1700 the practicalities of British topography and the consequent difficulties of communication limited people's horizons and made regional identity and variation very strong. Those on the West coasts would find it eas-ier to be in regular contact with Ireland than with London, while those near the South coast might know Normandy more intimately than Scotland. The Iron Age peoples of Britain were surely no more unified or uniform. To understand the Iron Age British, we must start at the local scale.

LIFE IN FARMS AND VILLAGES

Settlement forms varied greatly across the country. In some areas there were hamlets, and even quite substantial villages, as at Glastonbury, Somerset (fig. 58). Elsewhere the typical pattern was of dispersed farmsteads.

A common type was an individual house with ancillary structures in a yard enclosed by a fence or bank and ditch (figs. 61 and 64). Probably the bulk of the people lived in and worked from such farm-steads, which in many areas are associated with systems of ditches representing field and paddock boundaries, lanes and droveways. Social forms probably varied by region as much as the types of

60 *top* Aerial photograph of 'cropmarks' on the Yorkshire Wolds at Burton Fleming, East Yorkshire. By the Late Iron Age the settlement pattern in the area had evolved from scattered circular houses in a more or less open landscape to a more formal layout defined by ditches. Rectilinear enclosures lead off inter-connected trackways, suggesting increased population, changes in land-tenure and more intensive land use.

61 *above* Aerial photograph of 'cropmarks' in the Upper Thames valley revealing the buried remains of ditch systems of Iron Age settlements. Here the positions of 'banjo enclosures' – ditched farmyards with a droveway leading off – can be seen clearly, because the plants growing over the wetter fills of the long-silted ditches stay green while the rest of the crop yellows. Ashton Keynes, Wiltshire.

settlements, but most of these farms were presumably the homes of individual families, perhaps incorporating servants, slaves or other dependants.

The landscapes and especially the settlements which people construct both reflect and shape the patterns of their lives (figs. 62 and 63). The way space was laid out and used could tell us much about how people understood their world, and how they behaved in it. Much attention is currently being paid to questions such as gender roles and other divisions of activities, rights and responsibilities within communities. We still have much to learn about how to identify archaeological evidence for these aspects; current assumptions that, for example, textile production was a female role are little more than that. But can we at least identify what tasks were carried out, and where, in houses, outbuildings and yards?

Unfortunately, spatial distinctions within sites seem often to have been obliterated by many superimposed activities (such as repeated rebuilding of houses around the same spot, or continual redigging of ditches), or destruction by erosion. Nevertheless, artefacts found in and around houses, farmyards, villages, shrines, forts and fields give us other important clues to the lives of the men, women and children who dwelt there.

62 Reconstructions of Iron Age round-houses at Butser Ancient Farm, Hampshire. The house from Longbridge-Deverill-Cowdown, Wiltshire (left) is the largest known; most were like the more modest house beyond. British roundhouses were usually of timber, wattle and daub, presumably with thatched roofs. In areas where geology permitted or demanded, unmortared stone walls were used.

Recent research is detecting the cultural logic of the way settlements were laid out. Most roundhouses face between south and east, which hitherto was explained in terms of shelter from prevailing winds. A detailed study of house orientation suggests that many were aligned on the rising sun, particularly at the midwinter solstice or one of the equinoxes. Further, site enclosure ditches may often follow similar rules, with carefully orientated entrances.

63 Interior of a reconstructed Iron Age roundhouse at Cranborne, Dorset. Did they really look like this? Some Iron Age buildings are clearly dwelling houses, with internal hearths, but floors are rarely preserved and so detail of internal layout is rare. Others apparently served as workshops or stores. The circular shape will have affected and reflected the structure and lifestyle of the families which lived in them; round houses 'work' very differently from rectangular buildings.

Insulated with a thick thatched roof and heated by the central hearth, these could have been sophisticated and comfortable dwellings; it is inappropriate to compare them with Greco-Roman aristocratic residences, since it seems that the Britons, and other northern peoples, chose to invest their wealth and artistic skills in portable objects rather than architecture. This contrasts with the Roman world, where the wealthy invested in buildings, public and private, more than in artefacts.

RUBBISH AND RITUAL

Archaeologists have always assumed that the fragments of pottery, bone, and occasionally metal and other materials we find buried in ditches, pits, and post-sockets – which are all that remain of most Iron Age settlements – are simple accumulations of domestic rubbish, and are therefore direct, if partial, evidence for the routine activities of those who lived there. The material was seen as simply the discarded debris of activities like preparation and consumption of food, and production of clothing, domestic tools and utensils. Recent research on sites like Winnall Down and Danebury (Hampshire; fig. 65) has suggested that this apparently common-sense view is rarely – perhaps almost never – the case, at least for the Middle Iron Age of Wessex.

At such places, material was carefully selected and placed in the ground in regular ways, at highly infrequent intervals – a food-storage pit (fig. 66) was carefully filled in only once every decade or so. This is hardly routine rubbish disposal, and so the contents are not representative of daily life. What was the purpose of this 'structured deposition'? The pit-fills often include elements best interpreted as offerings, including animal skeletons or even human remains. Such deposits seem to be the product of ceremonies, including feasts. Do these acts of burial represent rites of thanks and propitiation of earth-gods who had protected foodstuffs while buried underground? They at least reflect the connections people made between themselves and domestic and wild animals, plants, and perhaps ancestors and the powers of the Earth, and the actions they believed necessary to ensure the continuity of life. They hint at forgotten belief-systems quite alien to our own, an aspect of what some archaeologists call the 'otherness' of the Iron Age.

(But what, then, happened to the routine refuse which all human communities produce? Probably it was dumped in manuring on the fields, and has been obliterated by time, weathering, and the churning of the plough.)

It seems that the functions which in our culture are divided up according to distinctions such as religious : secular, or military : civilian, all took place together in and around 'domestic' settlements. Disposal of the dead, religious rites, war and food production were all part of daily life, and not much separated out into special places (and, were probably not the preserve of specialist classes) at least until the Late Iron Age in the South.

64 Gussage-All-Saints, Dorset, under excavation. This was a fairly typical southern farmstead site, where little more than backfilled pits and boundary ditches survive. It is now evident that the thousands of settlements other than hillforts have mostly been flattened by later agriculture, with exceptions in protected areas like Salisbury plain, where a few still survive as earthworks. One of the pits produced manufacturing debris for chariot harness fittings (see fig. 48).

65 Danebury, Hampshire, the most extensively explored of all British hillforts. The outlines of the ramparts can be made out beneath the modern tree cover. Barry Cunliffe's excavation of large areas of the 4 ha. (10 acre) interior have revealed a well ordered pattern of roadways, houses (mostly in the lee of the rampart), post-built structures believed to be granaries, and hundreds of pits cut into the chalk of the hilltop.

CHANGING LANDSCAPES, CHANGING SOCIETIES

Despite the deceptive, apparent timelessness of ancient agriculture, Iron Age Britain was far from being an unchanging landscape, physically or socially. In fact, farming regimes changed profoundly in later prehistory.

Everywhere the environment could support it, a landscape of arable, pasture and managed woodland, dotted with farmsteads or hamlets and ditched field systems, was to be seen during the last centuries BC. This pattern has its roots deep in the Bronze Age, when the first round-house settlements appeared. Around the beginning of the Iron Age, many more permanent settlements, and new boundary systems were created – surely to do with control of the land and food production.

Individual settlements seem to represent the families and local communities which were the basic building blocks of larger polities. The Middle Iron Age was typified by small-scale societies, with at most minor local nobilities. East Yorkshire, for example, lacks identifiable strongholds or elite residences, although the cemeteries suggest important rank divisions (see p. 67). Elsewhere, absence of large settlements or of evidence for more than basic exchange of essential goods implies societies always remained small-scale, with little over-arching social organisation; settlements were semi-independent, and largely self-sufficient. Such societies may have been relatively egalitarian, but there were probably always dominant families or individuals.

Yet some areas exhibited radical social developments. For instance, hillforts were a transient phenomenon in many places and, even where they lasted for centuries, they reveal complex histories. This implies social change, as recent work at sites like Danebury has shown (fig. 65). Many societies underwent extensive reorganisation, beginning in the Middle Iron Age; Britain in 200 BC was a very different place from that which Caesar described a few generations later. Overall, the message is one of profound long-term change, with societies in central southern and south-eastern England mutating faster and further than those in the West or far North. By the Late Iron Age, southern societies had become much more elaborate, coalescing into larger units with more marked distinctions between ranks, and the emergence of kingship (p. 82). The result was the patchwork of diverse groupings which the Romans encountered.

It is hardly surprising that such social ferment involved violence within and between these communities, but what were its nature, roles and extent?

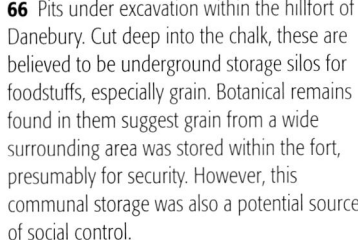

66 Pits under excavation within the hillfort of Danebury. Cut deep into the chalk, these are believed to be underground storage silos for foodstuffs, especially grain. Botanical remains found in them suggest grain from a wide surrounding area was stored within the fort, presumably for security. However, this communal storage was also a potential source of social control.

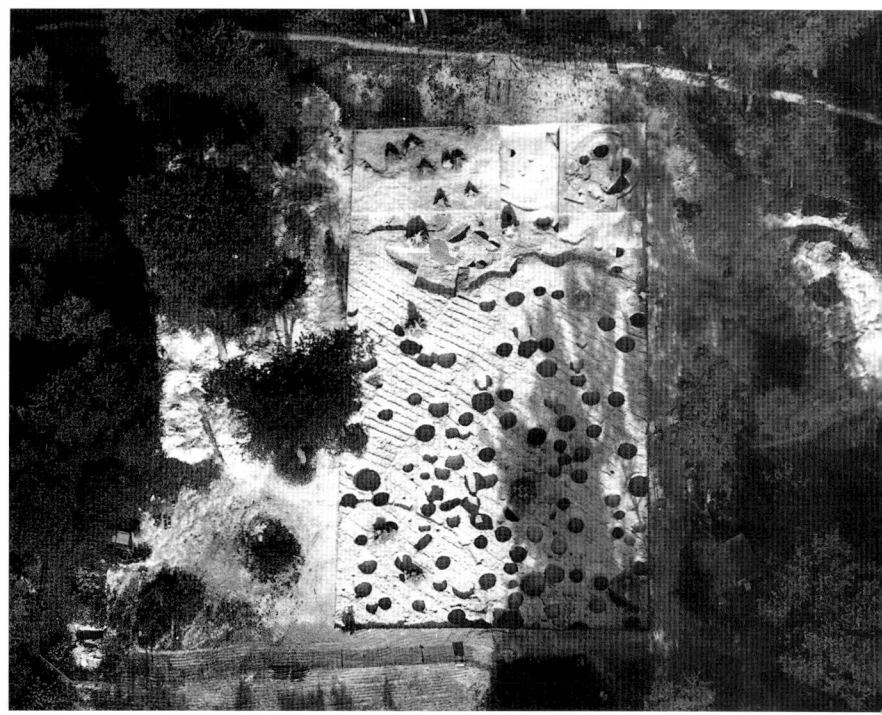

WAR AND VIOLENCE

Modern Western societies distinguish sharply between military and civilian, and between states of war and peace. But in early republican Rome, among propertied citizens war was an aspect of regular life, a short period of military service being a routine part of the annual cycle and accepted as normal. Warfare is prominent in the Classical texts on Britain, an impression seemingly confirmed by numerous hillforts, and finds of splendid arms. On the other hand, Diodorus, writing soon after the time of Caesar, says intertribal relations were for the most part peaceful. What, then, was the place of martial violence before contact with Rome?

Archaeology suggests weapons were common, but also valued for practical and symbolic purposes other than war. The basic armament of spear and shield could have been used for hunting, and as a marker of free manhood. The lavish, impractical design of some weapons suggests they were more for display than combat – although societies which prize weapons use them too (fig. 67). Nevertheless, skeletal evidence for inter-personal violence is ambiguous. Healed wounds on bones are the most convincing testimony (p. 21). 'Severed heads' from pits, ditches and rivers may represent funerary rites rather than trophy-taking.

The ambiguity of the evidence allows wide latitude for interpretation, and may appear equally consistent with widespread carnage or less actual fighting than macho display. We may imagine fluctuating levels of armed violence ranging from personal and clan feuds to wars between polities, mostly small-scale, and involving skirmishing, booty-raiding, and duels. Such conflicts might produce a lot of noise, but few casualties. There were evidently social mechanisms constraining armed conflict, since it did not prevent the continued growth and flourishing of British societies.

THE CHANGING FACE OF WARFARE

The Late Bronze Age was apparently a time of war; at least, some groups invested in fine weapons for military and ceremonial display. Deposition, if not the use, of such arms ceased around the start of the Iron Age. Possibly a nobility had established power based on control of scarce sources of copper and tin, but their power collapsed when the use of widely-available iron ores was learned from the Continent.

In any case, the coming of iron also saw the building of the first hillforts in many regions, perhaps in response to increasing insecurity as growing populations competed for control of limited farming lands. Previously scattered communities, it seems, were coming together for mutual support, coalescing into a mosaic of petty chiefdoms. Hillforts do not necessarily imply a warrior aristocracy; perhaps they suggest the opposite: an emphasis on communal defence.

67 The shield from the Thames gravels found at Chertsey, Surrey, in 1984. It reflects the elegant shape of wooden shields known from the European La Tène period. However, made entirely of yellowish copper alloy, this example is surely a display piece, probably hurled into the Thames for ceremonial reasons. Fourth century BC. L. 836 mm.

There is little sign of a well-defined warrior class, even in the hillfort-dominated Wessex of the sixth to second centuries BC.

Nevertheless, the concentration of people and resources in hillforts may have created the circumstances for the accumulation of power in the hands of the ambitious, leading to the gradual appearance of nobles who primarily presented themselves as warriors defending the community.

Weapons were clearly in use throughout the Iron Age, although expensive arms like swords, and especially helmets and body-armour, seem more a feature of the later period. The rise of the specialist warrior was connected with the rise of larger, more hierarchical societies in the later Iron Age.

68 A pair of linch-pins from the vehicle burial at Kirkburn, East Yorkshire. These square shanked iron pins with cast bronze ends secured the wheels onto the axle. The elaborate decoration reveals the meticulous craftsmanship lavished on high-status possessions. The triskele motifs on the cap and foot spiral in opposite directions but this fact was only noticeable when the cart was being completed or dismantled: such attention to detail is astonishing. Third century BC. L. 188 mm.

Much of the evidence for Late Iron Age finery, usually equated with warrior aristocrats, comes from areas without hillforts, or from areas where hillforts had been abandoned (figs. 68 and 69). In these zones there is growing evidence for exchange with the Continent. Perhaps the real source of noble power was forcible control of the flow of goods, especially highly valued imports, rather than war itself, although the wealth accrued was shown off in largely military forms.

The evidence for big changes in the Middle Iron Age South suggests that the substantial polities which Caesar encountered were quite a recent development. Archaeology hints at evolving military organisation and changing scales of war. With the growth of more centralised power, it may be that a pattern of fewer wars prevailed, and so could be described as general peace. Yet when wars happened, in a more directed way between larger groupings, they were probably on a larger scale, and are likely to have been more destructive.

BRITISH SOCIETIES AND THE CELTIC CONTINENT

Evidence for the structure of British societies and not least the archaeology of war, is clearly related to that of Gaul. The Chertsey shield shows continental inspiration in its elegant oval outline and spindle boss, but such bronze, or at least bronze-faced, construction is a British speciality, as is the Deal warrior's shield-shape (fig. 24). British sword types, for instance, show strong La Tène influence, but also exhibit equally strong regional traditions within the island (figs. 7 and 45).

Certainly, there are clear signs of cross-Channel contact. There are strong similarities of building forms between Brittany and Cornwall, and of hillfort construction techniques in southern Britain and Normandy. Yet the most fundamental cultural patterns, such as pottery traditions and the forms of houses, derive essentially from indigenous Late Bronze Age traditions; British roundhouses find their affiliations in Ireland and on the Atlantic fringes of Europe, and contrast strongly with the rectilinear architecture of the heartlands of the continental La Tène culture. British Iron Age societies grew primarily from local, Bronze Age roots.

The most striking similarities between British and Gaulish archaeology are at the level of nobilities – particularly in weapons and art – and are perhaps best explained by political and kinship links, and individual mobility between these elites. Such groups, probably responsible for establishing by military power the historically-attested polities of the Late Iron Age, may well have named them too. This could account for the cross-Channel commonality of a number of 'tribal' names, without the need to infer large-scale migrations; the *Parisi*, *Belgae*, *Brigantes* and not least the *Atrebates* all have continental cognates. The British Atrebates were ruled, and quite probably created, by Commius, an exile to Britain who was a noble of the Gallic Atrebates with personal links to the peoples of the island.

The scale and nature of cross-Channel similarities, then, suggest contacts between near neighbours, and not waves of invasion from a hypothetical Central European 'Celtic homeland'.

69 A set of bronze harness fittings for a two-horse vehicle, probably a war-chariot, from the Polden Hill hoard. This comprises a pair of snaffle-bits, and five terrets (rein-guides) from the yoke. Made by 'lost-wax' casting, the multiple-component, articulated bits are a *tour-de-force* of the smith's skills. First century AD. L. of bridle-bits 220 and 223 mm.

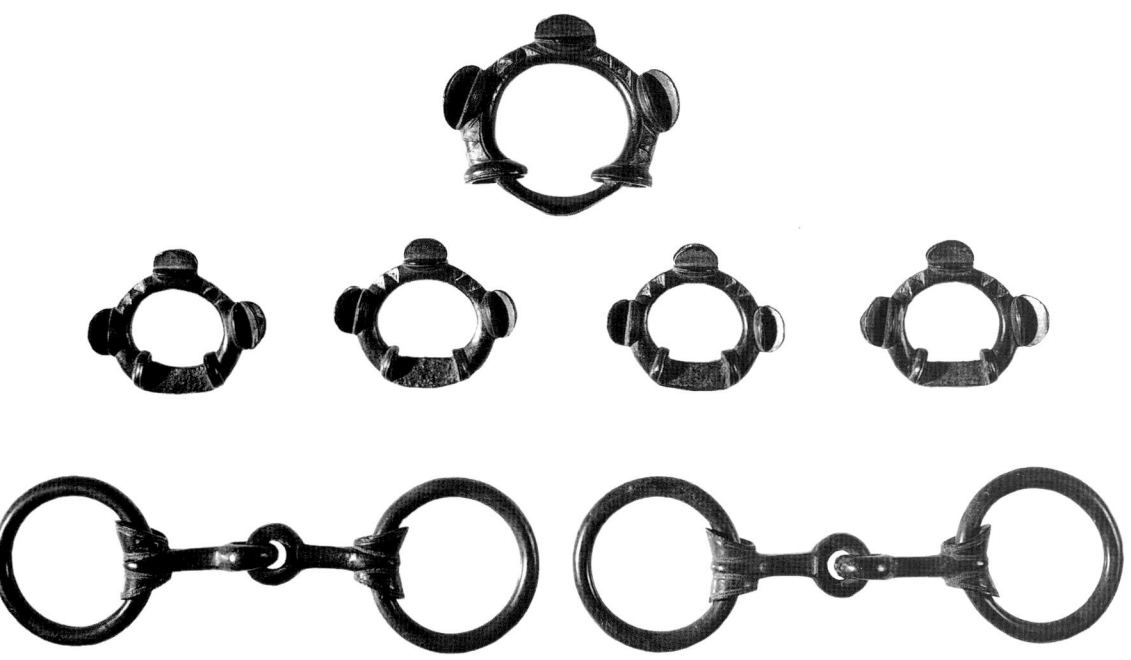

5 Rituals of life and death

The gods of the ancient Britons are elusive, as are their famous Druidical priests, at least archaeologically. Physical remains thought to represent religious and ritual activity are often encountered, but are hard to interpret. Water offerings and, more recently, the identification of 'structured deposition' in pits, are good examples. Burials, formal and apparently informal, can reveal details of rites, and hint at systems of belief.

Britons did not personify their gods in stone or bronze as did Greeks and Romans. A handful of wooden human figures recovered from wetlands are simple totem figures with no recognisable iconography. No so-called 'Celtic head' in stone is from a secure pre-Roman context. Stone sculpture was introduced to Britain by the Romans. However, there are human heads depicted on sword-hilts (fig. 18), which represent a major change over earlier British avoidance of depictions of the human form (figs. 70, 71). Perhaps this change, certainly of Gallic inspiration, reflects deeper innovations in British religious belief, and the way supernatural beings were conceived.

For the gods themselves, we are heavily dependent on Classical texts, which give some details of the beliefs of the Britons and more extensive information about the similar religions of the Gauls. These texts are often quite hostile, particularly regarding the Druids. Nevertheless, they at least record that the Gauls worshipped spirits of Nature with open-air rites, and believed in an afterlife.

Native British gods lived on under Roman rule, and some of their names are recorded in Latin inscriptions, but we can say little with confidence of their powers and attributes, still less of their mythology or Iron Age modes of worship. It seems clear at least that the Britons had no common pantheon of deities with defined powers, but myriad deities of the tribe, and of places.

DRUIDS

The Gauls told Caesar that Druidism originated in Britain, and was later introduced to Gaul. Highly learned men, often trained in Britain, Gallic Druids preserved traditional beliefs and rituals, and studied omens. Strabo recorded their alleged belief that: 'men's souls and the universe are indestructible, although at times fire and water may prevail', and they were said to believe in reincarnation. Tacitus accused British Druids of wholesale butchery of captives and using

70 *right* Hollow masks in sheet bronze, representing two highly stylised male faces complete with long curled moustaches, and the face of a horse with a rather lugubrious expression. They were found together with a vast collection of damaged horse-harness and weaponry within the Iron Age earthworks at Stanwick, Melsonby, North Yorkshire. The hoard was buried in the first century AD. L. of horse mask 100 mm.

71 *below* A gold torc terminal found at Snettisham, Norfolk. The highly stylised face-motif with its prominent almond-shaped eyes peers out from repoussé scrolls which encircle the neck-ring. Third century BC. L. of face 21 mm.

72 An iron scabbard ornamented with the 'dragon pair' motif which may actually represent birds with open beaks. It was dredged from the Thames with another example in the nineteenth century. Third century BC. W. 51 mm.

Opposite page
73 *top* A cast bronze knife which resembles the shape of a bird. Found by chance at St Stephens, Hertfordshire. Second century BC. L. 110 mm.
74 *right* A xero-radiograph of the bronze shield boss found in the nineteenth century at Ratcliffe-on-Soar, Nottinghamshire, but only correctly identified in 1994. The complex interlinked bird-motifs were executed with supreme skill. The design is characteristic of the fourth century BC. Diam. 135 mm.
75 *far right* Sheet bronze scabbard containing an iron sword from the river Lark near Isleham, Cambridgeshire. Such water offerings reflect a pattern of religious ritual shared not only with the Irish, and Continental Celts, but with the early Germans and the Classical world. First century BC. L. 767 mm.

their entrails for divining. Druids are archaeologically elusive, but Lindow Man may corroborate their involvement in human sacrifice. Four methods of inflicting death can be distinguished: his skull was smashed, he was garrotted and then his throat was cut, presumably to let blood. The body was then sunk in a stagnant pool, probably a symbolic drowning. He also had mistletoe pollen in his stomach. Pliny describes the ceremonial cutting of mistletoe for use in association with Druidical sacrifices of animals, so the presence of pollen from this plant in Lindow Man's stomach is tantalising, but inconclusive, evidence that he was a victim of Druidical rites. Nevertheless, the Druids' political power in war and peacemaking, and not human sacrifice, was probably the real reason Rome sought to destroy them.

PLACES OF RITUAL

For many of the peoples of Iron Age Britain, religious rites took place not in special sanctuaries, but in and around their dwellings, and in natural settings, notably rivers and pools.

River dredging in the nineteenth century resulted in the recovery of quantities of weapons of Bronze and Iron Age date. At first such finds were interpreted as losses in battle, but now deliberate deposition is the preferred explanation. It is assumed that masterpieces of the metal-worker's art like the Battersea, Chertsey and Witham shields and the Thames 'helmet' were ceremonially cast into rivers. Marvellous but scarcely functional examples of the bronze-smith's art, they may have been produced as ceremonial artefacts for eventual sacrifice in private or public rituals (figs. 12, 67, 72, 74 and 75).

Square double-ditched enclosures, totally different in shape to domestic settlements, have been interpreted as temples. One underlay the Romano-British temple on Hayling Island, Hampshire (fig. 82). Offerings such as brooches and weapons, but no precious metals or torcs, were excavated within its precincts. Such sanctuaries belong to the Late Iron Age South.

Recently, archaeologists have realised that there is probably a religious component for many discoveries hitherto explained in practical terms. For example, buried hoards of valuable objects like currency bars or torcs may not just be secure caches, but offerings to, or at least under the protection of, spiritual powers. We have already seen 'structured deposition' in pits, surely ceremonial in nature, sometimes incorporating human remains. And of course treatment of the dead is itself one of the most important aspects of ritual.

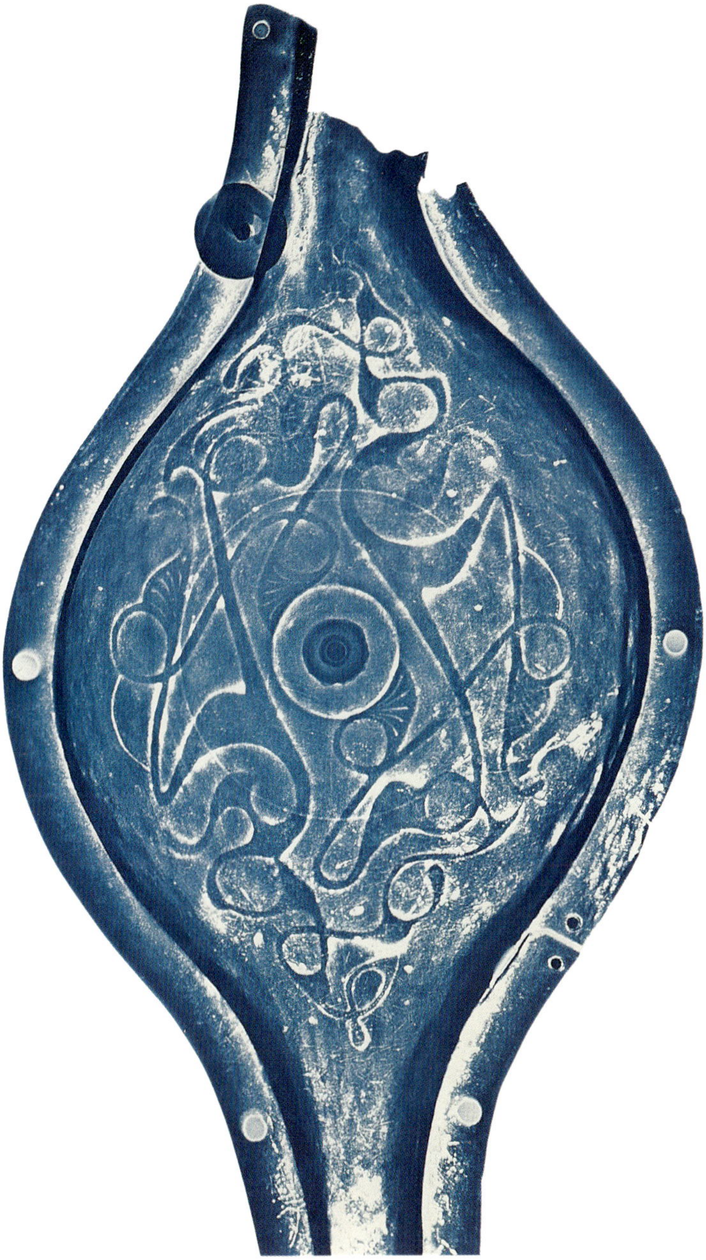

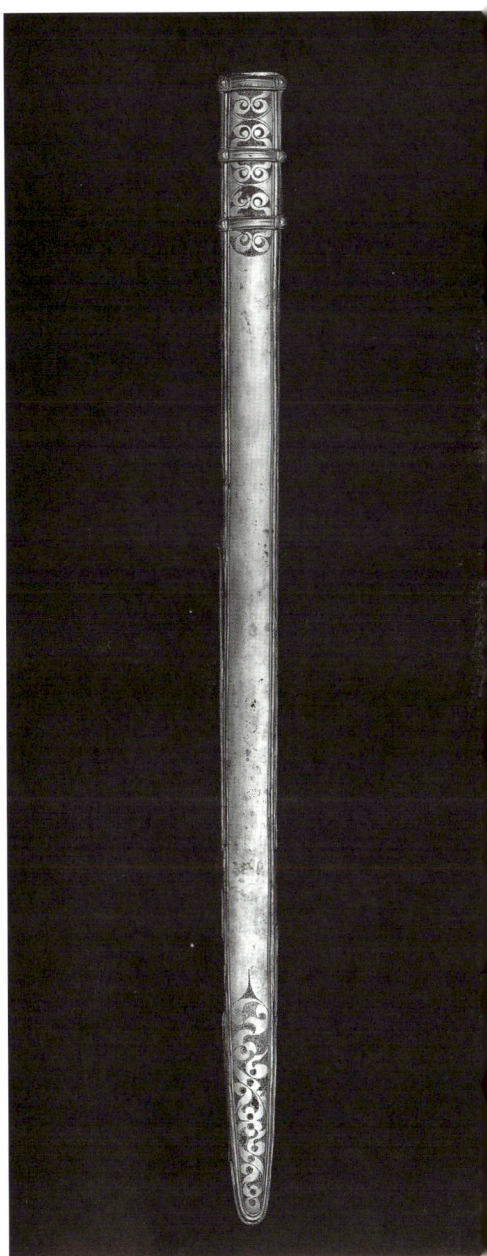

76 A group of eleven square ditched barrows in an area of the Burton Fleming Cemetery, East Yorkshire. The barrows are over 10 m square. Their regular shape and the central position of the grave in each denote reasonably accurate measurement. They are totally at variance with the typical circular ground-plan of contemporary houses.

RITES FOR THE DEAD

Burials in Britain exhibited strong regional traditions from the Middle Iron Age, with widespread change, and new rituals appearing, towards the end of the period. When in the fourth century BC the burial rite of inhumation in formal cemeteries was introduced in Deal, Kent, and East Yorkshire, it broke with a tradition lasting over 700 years where the disposal of the dead left no detectable archaeological trace. Perhaps bodies were disposed of by exposure to remove the flesh, and the scattering and destruction of bones on the surface. Such burials as took place were limited to inhumation within settlements, typically within a storage pit as it went out of use. By the time of Caesar's invasions in 55 and 54 BC inhumation had been widely if sporadically practised in lowland Britain. However, a continental-style cremation rite had already been introduced to parts of south-eastern Britain.

Pit burials are inhumations in pits scattered within a settlement, not concentrated in consecrated ground outside. Those at Danebury hillfort have little in common with contemporary cemeteries in East Yorkshire and Kent. Out of 300 deposits of human bone only 38 are more or less complete bodies. The remainder vary from single bones including almost complete skulls to skeletons with missing limbs. Five charnel deposits contain the jumbled bones from several different individuals. Correlating age at death with the completeness of the skeleton suggests that children were preferred for rituals leading to partial dismemberment. In burial, little ceremony or dignity appears to have been accorded to the remains. The poor diet of half of the children and a quarter of the adults may reflect unfree status.

CEMETERIES OF THE MIDDLE IRON AGE

More or less contemporary Middle Iron Age cemeteries at Deal, Kent and in East Yorkshire illustrate something of the diversity in inhumation burial rites in Britain. At Deal graves are haphazardly arranged on a loosely south-west to north-east orientation, in two small groups apparently sited with reference to a prominent Bronze Age round barrow and with no surviving boundary. In East Yorkshire cemeteries of the so-called 'Arras Culture', named after the site of the first cemetery to be excavated outside Market Weighton, are extensive and large, some containing more than 500 graves, and with clearly defined boundaries (fig. 76). The rectangular grave was orientated north to south at the centre of a square ditched barrow: existing burials were respected by later interments.

In both areas the corpse was treated with respect and maintained intact throughout: it was not subjected to defleshing by a long period of exposure, nor dismembered. Coffins were not used. In Yorkshire the body lay on its side in the foetal position, head to the north and facing the rising sun. Later the orientation was changed to east-west, with head to the east, and the position was extended and supine. In Kent the body was extended, supine, head usually to the south, as was the practice in cemeteries in Gaul.

Children and adults, females and males were buried in the same cemeteries. However complex the ceremonies preceding burial, over half the bodies are without any surviving offering which might denote particular beliefs, occupation, wealth or status. The remaining minority can be variously grouped according to different criteria including the number and function of the surviving grave goods.

In the cemeteries of the Arras Culture of East Yorkshire are seventeen burials of women and men assumed to be the leaders of their community, because they were interred with two-wheeled vehicles (fig. 77). Chain-mail at Kirkburn and swords at Wetwang provide support for the original interpretation of the vehicle as a war-chariot. Females buried with vehicles at Arras and Wetwang each have an

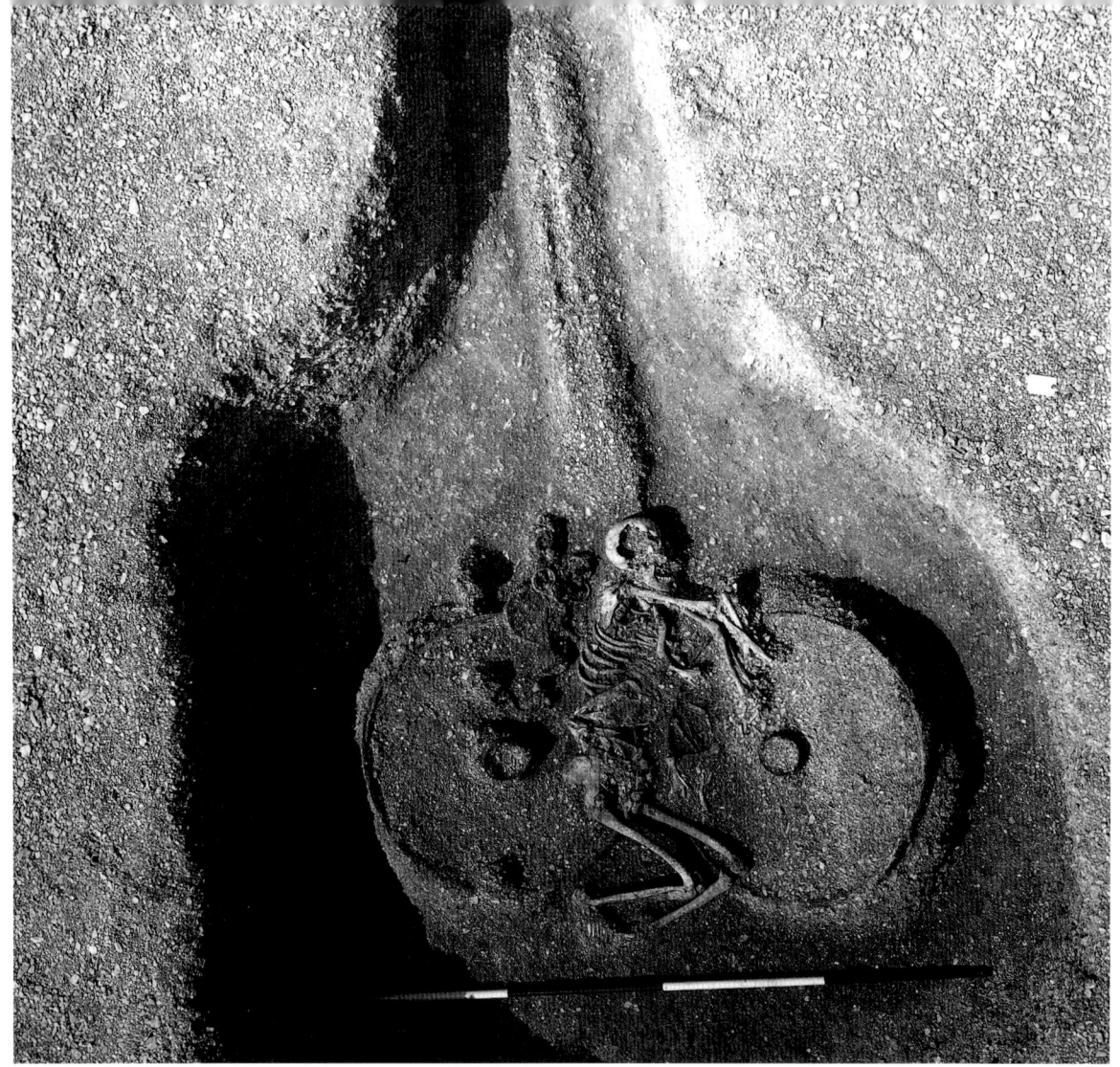

77 One of the vehicle burials of the third century BC excavated at Wetwang Slack, East Yorkshire. The wheels were removed and placed on the floor of the grave with the corpse of a woman positioned between them. The body of the vehicle was upturned and used as a cover. During excavation the remains of such burials typically resemble a 'bicycle'.

iron mirror. Mirrors were as significant for women as swords were for men. Although not common, they occur in burials in southern Britain from the fourth century BC until the late first century AD (fig. 43). While it seems improbable that either woman fought in battle, like Boudica they may have attended and encouraged the warriors. The Wetwang female was certainly flanked in death by graves of males armed with swords.

Perhaps next in status were men buried with swords – all are over the age of 17 years but only one had survived to 45 years. Spears or javelins tipped with iron and bone points were used in the most violent and macabre rite for which evidence survives in the Yorkshire cemeteries. They were thrust into a shield lying over the corpse, perhaps even directly into the body, as it lay in the grave. Such a ritual may have recorded battles bravely fought.

Other finds – single pots, metal pins, brooches, bangles, glass beads, iron knives and tools – give few obvious insights into the lives or

78 *right* The grave of a young woman buried in the Rudston cemetery, East Yorkshire, in a tightly crouched position, with her head to the north and facing the rising sun. She cradles a simple handmade pot in her arms. The pot contains a bone – the front left humerus of a sheep – which represents one of the most puzzling features of the ritual for only this bone occurs in such graves. It seems to be a symbol of a peaceful existence because it is not found in weapon burials.

79 *below* Finds from one of the 'richest' burials in the Rudston cemetery, dating to the third century BC. The simple and shapeless handmade pot with its coarse rock temper clearly visible is typical: when buried it already lacked a piece of the rim. The flat-bowed brooch was made of single piece of iron wire twisted into shape. The skeleton was wearing a broad bangle of finely polished jet and so may be that of a woman, but it was too fragmentary to be securely identified. H. of pot 180 mm.

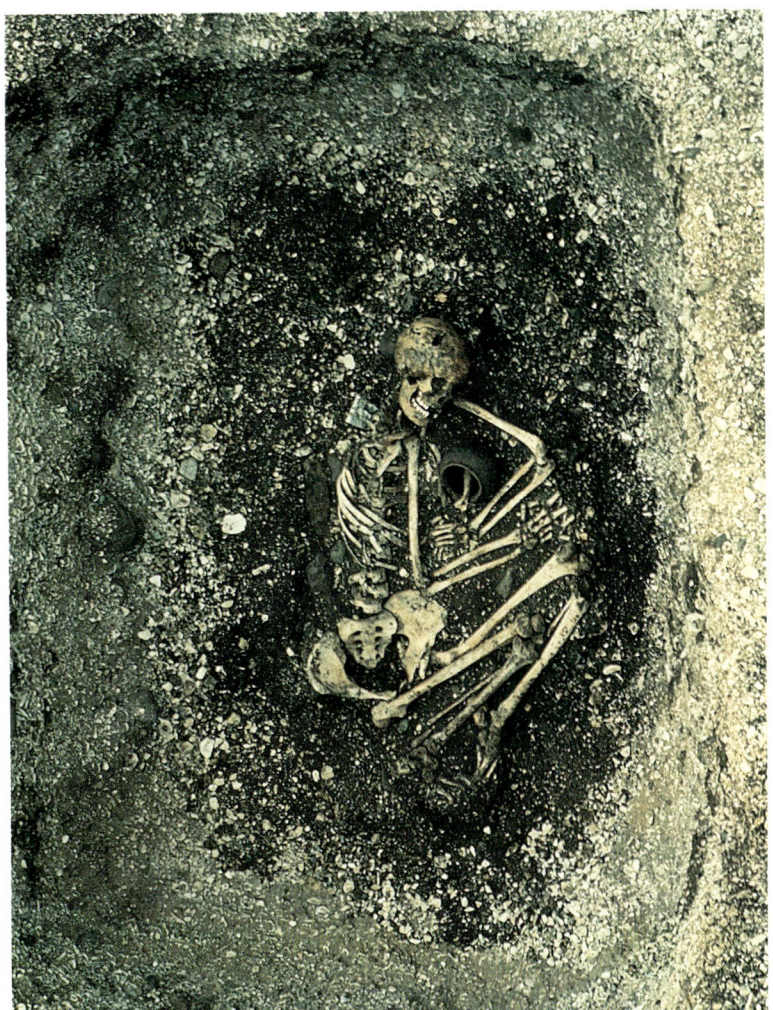

beliefs of the dead or the living who interred them. Small handmade pots are the single most common offering in female and male graves in the Rudston–Burton Fleming cemetery, East Yorkshire. They are associated with an intriguing ritual: twenty-nine pots contained an animal bone, always the left front leg of a sheep (fig. 78 and 79). Perhaps this was the portion of the burial feast ceremonially reserved for the deceased person. It was a strictly localised ritual, absent from a large cemetery only 25 km away, an illustration of the diversity, and highly localised scale of cultural life among British societies.

We do not know if the entire population of a community qualified for full burial rites. Around the vehicle burials at Kirkburn and Garton Station zoning of the cemeteries according to rank is a possibility. The males grouped around the vehicle graves were equipped with sword or spears. In the Rudston–Burton Fleming cemeteries the grouping of bodies exhibiting certain genetic-based skeletal abnormalities suggests that related family members were buried in close proximity.

80 A burial group dating to the mid-first century BC excavated at Alkham, Kent. The wooden bucket is encased with alternating bronze and iron bands while three ornamented rectangular plaques cover the feet. It contained the cremated bones of a male about 25 years old, with three brooches and part of a manicure set. The fine cordoned pots were thrown on a fast wheel and illustrate the skills achieved by potters using this recently introduced new technology. H. of tallest pot 300 mm.

CREMATION BURIALS OF THE LATE IRON AGE

Compared with the austerity of most inhumation burials, the cremation rite introduced into south-eastern Britain from Gaul early in the first century BC involved drinking, feasting and gaming, at least amongst the leaders of some communities. More ominous for their continued independence are imported luxury goods included among the offerings: in whatever manner wealthy southern Britons may have lived at this time, many were buried in the Gaulish style (figs. 80, 90). Their societies were spiralling closer to the Roman orbit.

The emphasis on feasting, drinking and gaming is more obvious in the graves found north of the Thames (figs. 90, 91). Italian wine, in amphorae each originally containing about 26 litres (over 150 modern glasses), played an obvious role in the funerary rite of 'Welwyn Burials', wealthy men cremated and buried in the mid- to late-first century BC in the region between the major *oppida* of *Verlamion* (St Albans, Hertfordshire) and *Camulodunum* (Colchester, Essex). Imported wine-drinking vessels in silver, bronze, glass and pottery were also interred (fig. 91).

Apparently representing wider sections of the population, the King Harry Lane Cemetery in the vicinity of *Verlamion*, the *oppidum* of the Catuvellauni, is the first extensive cremation cemetery of the Late Iron Age to be fully excavated (fig. 81). Beginning in the first decade of the first century AD over 450 burials were made within and between seven ditched enclosures over a period of fifty to sixty years, spanning the Roman conquest.

At the centre of each enclosure is a large rectangular grave with smaller graves encircling it. Beyond the enclosures are other 'family circles'. The central burials were the richest in grave goods; they are furnished with a selection of vessels for feasting and drinking, all in ceramic and most imported from Gaul, and a few personal items in metal (fig. 42). Some burials comprised only cremated bone.

81 Plan of part of the King Harry Lane Cemetery, St Albans, Hertfordshire, including the earliest enclosures which were established in the first decade of the first century AD and show 'family circle' grouping. Inhabitants of *Verlamion* continued to be buried there until after the Roman invasion.

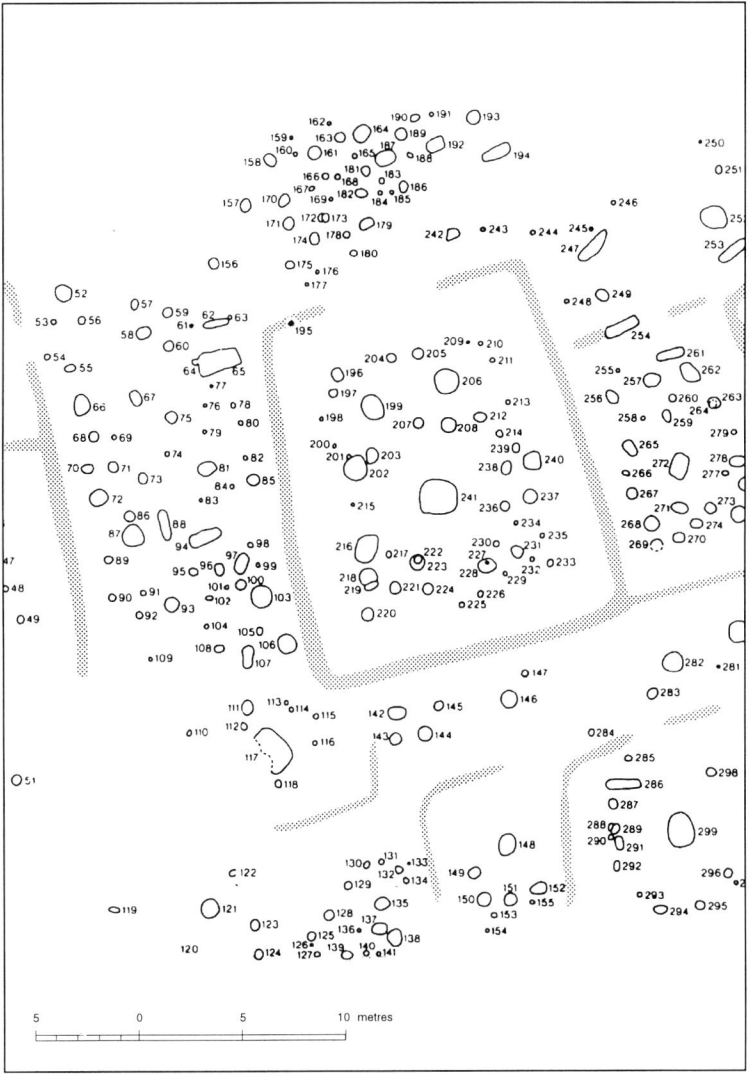

Over 800 pots were recovered. All are table-wares for eating and drinking, with no cooking-pots or storage jars (fig. 83). The remaining grave goods were personal, mainly brooches, an occasional bangle, finger-ring, mirror, knife or razor. There are no weapons and few craft tools. The absence of weapons and all trappings of the warrior class which the Roman invaders encountered suggests they had separate burial rites, like the wealthy individuals in the Welwyn graves. The recent discovery of a very elaborate cremation burial, accompanied by a mail shirt, in a special enclosure at nearby Folly Lane, may confirm this.

BRITAIN AND GAUL

Superficially, the evidence for ritual activity in Britain seems dominated by influences which can be traced to the Continent. However, more detailed examination shows that, as with other aspects, the underlying pattern is one of substantial continuity from the Bronze Age, with significant but localised continental influences mostly in the South, growing in importance towards the end of the Iron Age. This is seen particularly clearly in funerary practices where, for most of Britain, the 'disappearing dead' represent a pattern continuing from the Late Bronze Age.

In contrast with clear burial evidence for Gallic migrants in Italy, British cemeteries provide little convincing testimony for substantial continental immigration during the Iron Age. The East Yorkshire cemeteries show some Gallic influence, with square barrows and vehicle burials, yet the Yorkshire graves differ in basic details of rite

82 Plan of the Late Iron Age religious enclosure which preceded the Roman temple at Hayling Island, Hampshire. The spatial distribution of iron weapons and bronze artefacts within the sanctuary demonstrate that there were designated areas for offerings of specific types or from people following specific occupations. The enclosure is roughly 23 m by 28 m.

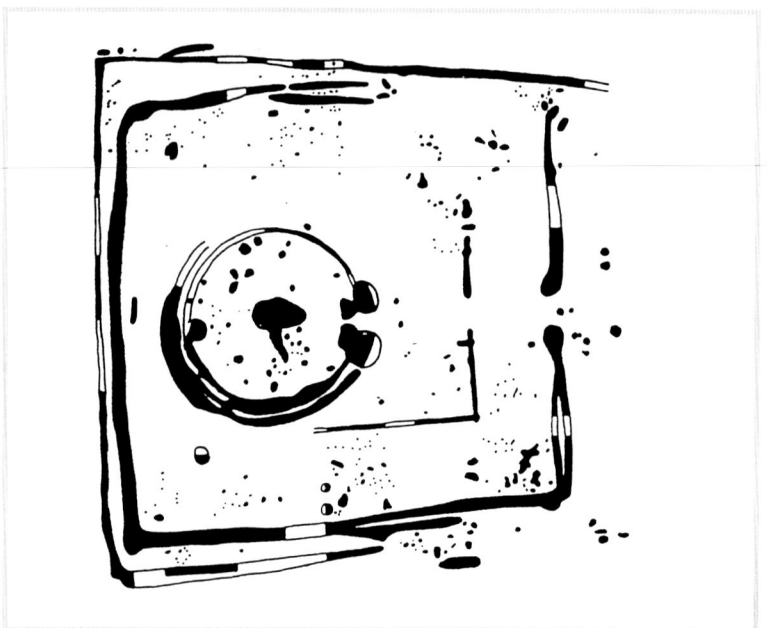

83 The head of this duck-shaped vessel forms a removable stopper so that it can be used for liquids. A potter living in or near *Verlamion* early in the first century AD made it using traditional methods and firing techniques but the inspiration for the shape and function was provided by imports from the Roman world. The duck was found in a burial in the King Harry Lane Cemetery. H. 220 mm.

– vehicles and bodies are disposed in different ways – and the grave-offerings are all of local manufacture. They contain only a single possible Gallic import, surprising if there had been a mass migration. The details are again less consistent with large population movements than with transmission of funerary fashions, perhaps through the movement of small groups of aristocrats. This may explain how, at least by Roman times, the Britons of East Yorkshire shared a tribal name with the Gallic *Parisi*.

The evidence, then, limited though it is, fits best with the idea of prolonged, intermittent cross-Channel contact, with adoption of fashions through exchange contacts, and some localised movement of people, of aristocratic groups as much as whole communities, around the southern and eastern coastal fringes. The appearance of Gallic-style cremation cemeteries of the Late Iron Age South may be explained in this way, and we have specific details of some Gallic immigration, including nobles like Commius (fig. 84). Temples like Hayling Island also belong to this 'Gallicising' trend.

The evidence for Druids, problematic though it is, at least serves to emphasise that the idea of British dependence on waves of ideas and fashions, if not migration, from a Continental Celtic 'core' is simplistic. Druidism was, we are told, a British export to Gaul. Cross-Channel exchange in religion, as in the secular realm, was a two-way process.

Change, contact and conquest

84 *above* A gold coin of Commius, the Gallic Atrebatan prince who, on falling out with Julius Caesar, fled to Britain and established himself as a local ruler. First century BC.

85 *below* The known tribal units of Britain in the first century AD, during the Late Iron Age and Roman conquest periods, based on documentary and numismatic evidence. These groupings seem to have been very dynamic and unstable; most of the tribal names listed by Caesar in 55 BC had gone by AD 43.

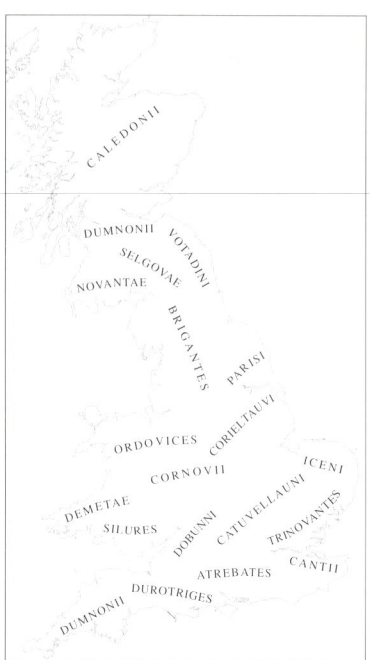

Britain underwent a period of profound change between the second century BC and the early centuries AD. It can be divided into three major phases: firstly, the time before Caesar's raids in 55 and 54 BC; secondly, the century or so between Caesar's bringing of Roman power to the shores of the English Channel, and the definitive invasion of Britain in AD 43; and lastly, Rome's attempt, only partially successful, to integrate Britain into the Empire.

The Late Iron Age was apparently the period of development of the larger 'tribal' polities, of more established kingship over large populations and tracts of territory (fig. 85). The appearance of the trappings of the proto-state, with increasing levels of wealth and ostentatious display by the few, were in turn intimately linked with increased degrees of contact with continental Europe. In the first instance, these connections were with the Gauls, and through them increasingly with the growing empire of the Roman Republic, which in the later second century BC had established itself in the south of France.

The changes in later Iron Age Britain can be seen as the result of a 'bow-wave' effect of initial contact with the expanding urban civilisation of the Mediterranean, the prelude to what, with hindsight, appears inevitable conquest by Rome. In Gaul, as military expansion brought Rome into contact with the peoples around the headwaters of the Rhône, so the flow of trade, and political and cultural influence helped to precipitate the formation of increasingly Romanised tribal states among the Eastern Gauls. This influence was felt in an attenuated form as far as Southern Britain, with Italian imports arriving via the Atlantic coast seaways. Once Gaul was conquered in the 50s BC, Britain was more directly exposed to Mediterranean culture, which is often implicitly credited with driving the pace of change. More realistically, Rome was less a prime mover than a catalyst. *Because of local changes already underway* aspects of Roman culture proved useful to some of the developing Gallic and, later, British polities – but not to others. The Gallic *Belgae*, the Northern Britons and the early Germans were still too different – in Roman eyes too barbarian – and were resistant to foreign ways.

LATE IRON AGE BRITAIN: DIVERGENT SOCIETIES

During the decades around 100 BC there were many signs of change, at least in the 'Lowland Zone'. The origins of the developments

86 The hillfort of Hod Hill, Dorset. Traces of the internal layout and locations of houses can still be made out. An active settlement at the time of the Claudian invasion, it was captured and a Roman fort inserted into one corner.

which gripped the South and East are hard to fathom, but they led to profound changes in the scale of life which saw much more than the gradual abandonment of hillforts. Unprecedented population growth was linked with intensification and improvement in agriculture; with the appearance of new kinds of artefacts, not least exotic foreign imports such as wine-jars, revealing the development of new trading and exchange networks; and with the development of wholly new settlement types. All this was linked to the crystallisation of larger and more complex societies.

The rest of the country was much less affected. Like all societies, those of the North and West continued to evolve but more slowly, and older, small-scale patterns of life persisted.

Archaeological survey now suggests many thousands of settlements in the Late Iron Age landscape, implying a population of several million by the Roman conquest. The regional patterns vary, and include villages and hamlets, with ditch-enclosed farmsteads predominating. Often associated with ditched field systems, such sites produce seeds from new crop varieties and bones from improved animal breeds. Intensification of agriculture was perhaps one response to growing competition for land, a pressure implied by expansion of cultivation onto poor soils.

Increasing population and agricultural production, with greater surpluses, permitted and perhaps demanded larger-scale social organ-

87 Iron 'currency bars', semi-finished iron prepared for distribution. The long shapes probably allowed the quality of the iron to be readily seen. Numerous hoards of these objects have been found widely distributed in southern Britain, but none from the North. These examples were found in hoards at Hod Hill, Dorset, Winchester, Hampshire and Malvern, Worcestershire. First century BC. L. of bar (far right) 800 mm.

88 A selection of bronze artefacts of Iron Age British origin from Hod Hill, including terrets (top) and tankard handles (bottom right). By comparison with Roman sites, Iron Age settlements usually produce few artefacts apart from bone and pottery; even the latter is sparse in many regions. Such fragmentary metal finds are relatively rare and rich discoveries; apart from ritual deposits, metal was usually recycled rather than buried. Second and first centuries BC. L. of handle (bottom right) 138 mm.

isation with more elaborate hierarchies. Larger polities, or at least the emergent nobilities which dominated them, engaged in more intensive trade, over longer distances, with a wider range of goods than ever before. Within Britain, for example, finds of iron 'currency bars' reflect the exchange of an important raw material in standardised quantities and qualities (fig. 87). On a larger scale, overseas political and economic contacts increased greatly, leading to a taste for foreign ways and goods both from neighbouring Gaul, and the Classical world beyond.

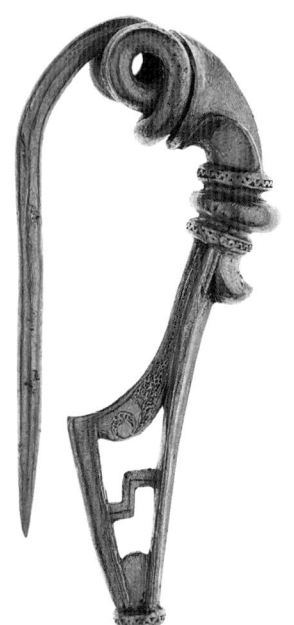

89 A gold fibula of the first century AD found near Market Rasen, Lincolnshire. Moulding on the bow and the prominent hook below produce the effect of a grotesque bird. A tiny motif was engraved on the catch-plate. L. 44 mm.

Finds of objects of foreign manufacture are of particular interest to archaeologists, not least because they can help to establish chronological links between the ranges of artefacts in use by different peoples at a given period. They also of course provide evidence for contacts, whether through trade, immigration or even invasion. Importations of new categories of object, particularly luxury goods, can indicate changes in the lifestyle of peoples or classes.

For the Iron Age, no certain finds of imported objects have been made in Britain which date much before 100 BC. Certainly, objects of earlier date reflect familiarity with continental fashions, but they are British reinterpretations; for example, certain dagger scabbards from the Thames are of continental form, but have a characteristically insular belt-loop (fig. 7).

Gaulish coins are amongst the earliest evidence of cross-channel exchange. The use of coinage was imitated, one of the earliest signs of 'Gallicisation' in Britain. The first British coins, struck in the second century BC, are gold and copy issues of the *Ambiani* of Northern Gaul. Early issues were very large denominations, surely not for routine commercial transactions, but for prestigious political and social interactions. The exchanges and payments represented by these coinages will have included political dealings at the highest levels, including forging of treaties, payment of tribute, ransom or dowries in dynastic marriages, and the hiring of mercenaries such as those Britons Caesar encountered in Gaul.

Early trade with the Mediterranean was dominated by the tribes of *Armorica* (Brittany). Hengistbury Head, Dorset, was probably the major port of trade in the earlier first century BC, when the earliest metal drinking-vessels and fragments of Italian wine-jars are concentrated towards the South-West.

Domestic pots from Brittany and Normandy are found on and around the Isle of Wight, while those at Deal in Kent are indistinguishable from pots produced in the Pas de Calais. In addition to trade, the quantities involved may suggest some Gallic settlement in British coastal districts (as Caesar later reported). In contrast, imported goods are entirely absent in the North and North-West. There were clearly marked regional differences in the extent and nature of these interactions.

THE LEGACY OF JULIUS CAESAR

Caesar's conquest of Gaul led to brief expeditions to Britain in 55 and 54 BC. Although dramatic and historically symbolic, they had little direct lasting impact on the British peoples. Far more significant in the long run was the fact that Caesar brought Roman government permanently to the shores of the English Channel. Thereafter Britain and Rome were no longer distant curiosities to one another, but shared a regular and growing commerce detailed by the geographer Strabo, and elucidated by archaeology. Strabo lists gold, cattle, hides, grain, hunting dogs and slaves as British exports. Earlier Gallic practice was to exchange slaves for wine, and indeed the archaeological evidence for imports is mostly for luxury goods, especially wine and drinking vessels. British slavery and slave-trading are probably attested by finds of chains for gangs of captives. Still, it is thought that the products of the land were the most important commodities, probably to supply Rome's Rhine garrisons. After Caesar, the more easterly distribution of Italian amphorae reveals the shifting of the principal axis of exchange to the Thames Valley–Rhineland route.

WINE, LUXURY IMPORTS AND THE DISPOSAL OF THE DEAD

Along with fine Gallic tablewares, Italian wine and drinking vessels played an important role in the burial rite of a group of wealthy males interred in the region north of the Thames in the decades after Caesar, the Welwyn burials (figs. 90 and 91). These tombs represent a major departure in the South; such formal burials, employing cremation of the dead and interment with imported goods, and the appearance of substantial formal cemeteries, are all wholly new features. Do these Gallic-style cremation graves represent immigrants,

90 Reconstruction of a Late Iron Age cremation burial from Baldock, Hertfordshire. The bronze cauldron contained the ashes of an adult male. He was accompanied by an Italian wine jar, a pair of iron fire-dogs, bronze bowls and two bronze-bound buckets. The handles of the latter were attached by fittings bearing human heads similar to that from the Aylesford bucket (*front cover*). Early first century BC. H. of firedogs 700 mm.

91 A selection of the luxury imports found chiefly in Late Iron Age cremations. Only inorganic items survive: gold jewellery, silver cups, bronze, glass and ceramic vessels. Organic materials – rich fabrics, perfumes, wine, olive oil and exotic foods – have long since perished. The latter were available, in small amounts, to a privileged few who enjoyed choice and variety more akin to life in the Mediterranean world and on a scale previously unknown in Britain. The choice of grave goods suggests that the dead intended to maintain in the afterlife the standards to which they were accustomed in life. 20 BC – AD 50. H. of white flagon 360 mm.

whether Gaulish nobles (such as the exile Commius, p. 74), or expatriate Gallic traders? Or are they the tombs of British nobles adopting increasingly Romanised Gaulish lifestyles? All could be represented.

These graves are part of a much wider range of revolutionary changes in the territories where they are found. Henceforth, after Caesar, the changes underway in the South are increasingly continental in flavour, as contacts grew ever closer with the culturally similar Gauls, and the different but fabulously rich and powerful Roman world. Some aspects of *Romanitas*, such as perhaps the use of Latin letters on coins, came directly, through imperial political contacts and trade. Others came via indirect means, through exchange, kin links and cultural contacts with the Britons' Gallic cousins, who were themselves forging a hybrid Romano-Celtic civilisation, especially in the early decades AD.

Although important, it is easy to overemphasise this highly visible Gallo-Roman strand. How far were societies motivated to 'Gallicise' by internal needs, and how far by the attraction of foreign examples? What was the interplay of these external influences with local processes which, as we have seen, were already at work?

In the Middle Iron Age, activities which we would distinguish between as sacred and profane all seem to have taken place on settlement sites. In the Late Iron Age South there was greater specialisation, with the appearance of separate shrines and formal cemeteries. Such changes surely reflect the development of more complex societies, with greater separation of functions, and the rise of specialised places, institutions and groups. The latter included priesthoods, apparently 'professional' warriors and a powerful nobility which flaunted its wealth, not least in the lavish 'Gallicising' burial rites discussed earlier. Currency use developed to include silver and base-metal issues as well as gold, and coins were now inscribed with the name of the issuing ruler and of the chief settlement (fig. 94).

These were all parts of a package of simultaneous changes in south-eastern Britain, which saw the development of several proto-states with centralised kingship, new royal power being associated with sprawling new city-like centres, now referred to as *oppida*.

In the last decades BC, a number of settlements of unprecedented nature and scale appeared in southern Britain. Of varied form, they were all rambling agglomerations of population, industrial production, trading activity and apparently governmental and religious functions. The best-known examples include *Verlamion* of the Catuvellauni (St Albans, Hertfordshire), *Calleva* of the Atrebates (Silchester, Berkshire), and *Camulodunon*, initially of the Trinovantes (Colchester, Essex). Although associated with impressive systems of earth banks, their primary function was not as strongholds – they

92 With a total of ten pots, over half imported from Italy and Gallia Belgica, Burial 346 was one of the richest cremation burials in the King Harry Lane Cemetery, St Albans, Hertfordshire. It was also one of the earliest, dating to the first quarter of the first century AD.

Cremation reflects a totally different attitude to the body. It was probably believed to release the spirit from the flesh. To burn the body properly the temperature in the (probably wood-fuelled) pyre had to reach at least 1200°C. After burning, the fragmented bone was collected for deposition in the grave, where it was heaped on the floor with the grave goods arranged around it, or placed in a container.

93 A selection of brass brooch-types imported into free Britain from occupied Gaul in the period AD 10–50. They were designed to be generally larger and have a more extensive area for ornament than surviving native types. From the King Harry Lane cemetery, Hertfordshire. L. of horizontal brooch 50 mm.

were settlements approaching urban status. Archaeologists refer to these sites by the Roman name of *oppidum*, 'town', which Caesar applied to the similar proto-cities of Gaul. These are the places named on the coins, which also bear the names of kings.

At the same time, proximity to Roman power, and the model of Romanisation presented by Gaul, evidently encouraged in southern Britain a thirst for Roman and especially Gallo-Roman goods and imitations of them, seen for example in the cremation graves of the King Harry Lane cemetery, outside *Verlamion* (figs. 91, 92 and 93). Glossy red Samian pottery and Gallo-Roman brooch types are found on rural sites all over the south within a generation of the Roman conquest. This represents significant proto-Romanisation of some of the southern British polities, particularly of their ruling classes. In important respects, these polities were becoming quite similar to the urban civilisations and kingdoms of the contemporary Mediterranean, and so ever more suitable for Roman conquest.

ROMAN INVASION

After several false starts, a Roman invasion force landed at last in AD 43, aiming finally to incorporate Britain into the Empire. While the immediate reason was the emperor Claudius's need for military

94 *below* Obverse of a bronze coin of the Catuvellauni. AD 1–40. The tribal capital was *Verlamion* (Roman *Verulamium*) recognised by the use of a mint mark VER on some coins.
95 *bottom* Reverse of a gold coin (*aureus*) of Claudius showing a triumphal arch, celebrating the conquest of Britain. The incorporation of the new province was the subject of a propagandistic extravaganza by the emperor.

prestige, Britain had long been on the agenda for conquest because the island, or at least the southern districts known to the Romans, was an attractive prize (fig. 95). It produced the agricultural surplus necessary for successful conquest and occupation, and consisted of fairly centralised political units capable of conversion into approximations of Classical city states, a strategy the Romans had successfully applied in turning much of Gaul into imperial provinces.

In the South, British culture was transformed. Romano-British society was not just an attenuated copy of Roman civilisation but, like those of many other frontier provinces, was a reinterpretation of it through native eyes, a genuine hybrid culture reflecting varying responses, and *degrees of predisposition*, to accept, adopt and adapt – or reject – aspects of Greco-Roman culture.

The North proved to be very different, its conquest and Romanisation much harder. Its generally small-scale societies had little use for the trappings of Mediterranean civilisation, which were primarily of interest to the wealthy nobilities of the South and East. Developed nobilities did not exist in the North and West – the land could not support the requisite dense populations and complex hierarchies. Also, the Roman army ground to a halt in this zone, military rule hindering the development of the semi-autonomous Romanised communities which characterised the successful provincial districts. Beyond the frontier zone, life continued largely, although by no means entirely, unaffected by Roman provincial culture.

The growing cultural divergence of the North and West from the South and East was reinforced under Rome. Crudely, the latter continued on a trajectory established in the last two centuries BC towards larger and more complex societies, although now heavily exposed to Classical influences. This led to the appearance of a new, hybrid Romanised society, integrated with the Empire, and perhaps so dependent on imperial connections that it did not survive the collapse of the Roman West in the fifth century AD, opening the way to the establishment of the immigrant, Germanic-speaking ancestral English.

Peoples in the North and West were largely impervious, or at least resistant, to Romanisation. Thereafter the political and cultural histories of the two zones were permanently on separate tracks. Long-term Roman political and military intervention in Caledonia (Scotland) may have precipitated the formation of one of the large new barbarian confederations which subsequently destroyed the Roman West: the Picts. In early medieval times the Picts and other Northern and Western groups underwent state-formation themselves, leading ultimately to a Britain divided between Germanic-speaking England on the one hand, and originally largely Celtic-speaking Wales and Scotland on the other.

Conclusion: Britain and the Celtic Iron Age

At the end of the twentieth century, the picture archaeology gives us of Iron Age Britain is one of a populous land, home to a patchwork of societies, artistically accomplished and often quite wealthy. These grew primarily out of the societies of Bronze Age Britain, yet with vital, if erratic, contributions and influences from continental Europe in the form of trade, kinship links, and pretty certainly some localised immigration, especially in the Late Iron Age South.

Perhaps the strongest messages drawn from the increasing wealth of information before us are the *strangeness* and the *diversity* of Iron Age Britain. Although these communities were in important senses ancestral to peoples of modern Britain, they were more different from us, more alien, than we had imagined. And the more we find out, the more varied and complex the Iron Age looks, and the more resistant to generalisation; Britain was an island of many distinctive and changing cultural identities, more sharply varied than the Welsh, English and Scots have been in recent centuries.

The search for the pre-Roman past of Britain began by seeing it through Greco-Roman eyes, and it saw barbarians. Early archaeology identified physical traces of these Britons, related them to their continental cousins, and labelled them all Celts. Considering the commonalities between Britons and their Irish and continental relatives provided the key to identifying the Ancient Britons archaeologically. Yet now we realise that this has been overplayed, and emphasis on common 'Celticness' generated a misleading presumption of fundamental uniformity, masking and suppressing the profound differences among the ancient peoples of the British Isles, and between them and the Celtic Continent. Forcing a range of disparate cultures into a predefined common 'Celtic' mould denies these vanished peoples any chance of a 'voice', or of our recognising their individuality and the levels of identity most important to them.

The Ancient Britons appear never to have called themselves Celts. Only we have decided to describe them so. Even 'British' as a common label may be anachronistic. The peoples of Britain may not have had a single collective name for themselves. It seems likely that, to most people living in the island, their 'tribal' identity was probably the highest level to have great significance, at least until the appearance of the serious external threat from Rome. Indeed common British national identity – as opposed to Scottish, Welsh or English – is a remarkably modern phenomenon, belonging especially

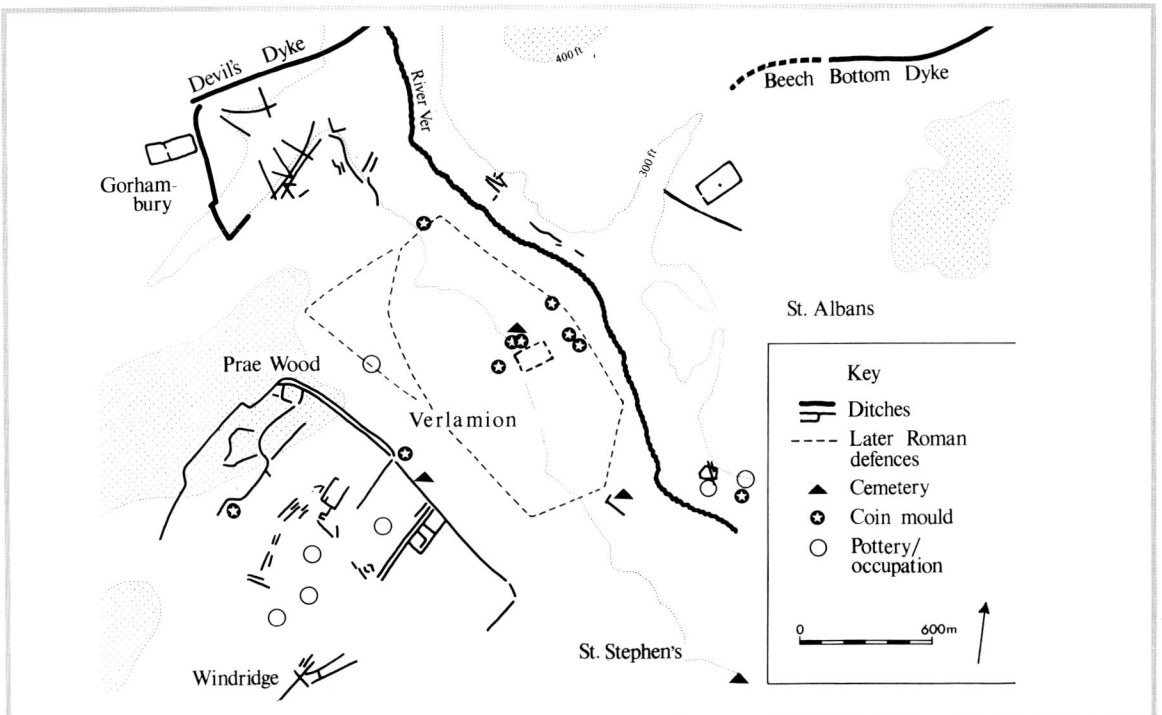

96 Plan of the *'oppidum'* of *Verlamion* in the early first century AD, forerunner of the Roman town of *Verulamium*. Unlike the enclosed Roman city (dotted line) which overlies and largely obscures it, the Iron Age settlement sprawled, but a number of distinctive zones have been identified, not least funerary zones, areas of industrial production, and probable aristocratic nuclei.

to the years following the Act of Union between Scotland and England/Wales in 1707. Throughout recorded history, there have always been multiple ethnic or political identities within the island, not uniform Britons, never mind generic Celts.

The Iron Age, then, is surely best considered in terms of a hierarchy of identities. Local ones were, we can reasonably infer, the most important to the peoples of the time. Britain was home to a group of developing societies related to their neighbours in Ireland and on the Continent, but also distinctive; 'Briton' is more a geographical than a cultural or political label. It may also still sometimes be useful to think of them as part of a wider world we choose to call 'Ancient Celtic'.

What does the future hold for the archaeology of Iron Age Britain? Current emphases on themes as diverse as gender roles and the new perspective of the 'otherness' of the period, will be pursued. Detailed studies of life on single settlements, and in small areas, will explore the richness of regional diversity, particularly to counteract the long-standing bias towards the seductive archaeological riches of the South, especially Wessex. All this will undoubtedly be supplemented by further chance discoveries of spectacular remains. The continuing explosion of knowledge is constantly bringing new insights into the lives of the peoples of Iron Age Britain, and the debate over the nature of their relationships to the peoples of contemporary continental Europe is sure to continue.

FURTHER READING

The following is a tiny selection from the vast literature on the field, and is intended to be a mix of basic texts and syntheses, books with special reference to the British Museum collections, and some leads into the newest perspectives on the subject. Many of the volumes below have copious bibliographies.

IRON AGE ARCHAEOLOGY AND THE QUESTION OF THE CELTS

M. Chapman, *The Celts: The Construction of a Myth*, Macmillan Press, Basingstoke, 1992

J. Collis, *The European Iron Age*, Batsford, London, 1984

P. Graves-Brown, S. Jones and C. Gamble (eds), *Cultural Identity and Archaeology: The Construction of European Communities*, Routledge, London and New York, 1996, especially chapters 8, 11 and 16

M. J. Green (ed.), *The Celtic World*, Routledge, London and New York, 1995

J. D. Hill, 'Can we recognise a different European past? A contrastive archaeology of later prehistoric settlements in Southern England', *Journal of European Archaeology*, 1 (1993) 57–75

S. James, *Exploring the World of the Celts*, Thames and Hudson, London and New York, 1993

V. Kruta, O. H. Frey, B. Raftery and M. Szabó, *The Celts*, Thames and Hudson, London and New York, 1991

J. J. Tierney, 'The Celtic Ethnography of Posidonius', *Proceedings of the Royal Irish Academy*, vol. 60, 1959–60, 189–275

IRON AGE BRITAIN AND IRELAND

T. C. Champion and J. R. Collis (eds) *The Iron Age in Britain and Ireland: recent trends*, J. R. Collis, Sheffield, 1996

B. Cunliffe, *Iron Age Britain*, Batsford/English Heritage, London 1995

B. Cunliffe, *Iron Age Communities in Britain*, 3rd edn, Routledge, London and New York, 1991

A. P. Fitzpatrick and E. L. Morris (eds), *The Iron Age in Wessex: Recent Work*, Association Française d'Étude de l'Age du Fer, 1994

A. Gwilt and C. C. Haselgrove, forthcoming 1996, *Reconstructing Iron Age Societies: New Approaches to the British Iron Age*, Oxbow Monograph 71, Oxbow Books, Oxford

Barry Raftery, *La Tène in Ireland: problems of origin and chronology*, Veröffentlichung des Vorgeschichtlichen Seminars Marburg 2, 1984

Barry Raftery, *Pagan Celtic Ireland: the enigma of the Irish Iron Age*, Thames and Hudson, London and New York, 1994

A. Ross, *Pagan Celtic Britain*, Routledge and Kegan Paul, London, 1967

THE PEOPLE

D. Brothwell, *The Bog Man and the Archaeology of People*, British Museum Publications, London, 1986

K. Parfitt, *Iron Age Burials from Mill Hill, Deal*, British Museum Press, London, 1995

F. B. Pyatt et al., 'Non isatis sed Vitrum or, The Colour of Lindow Man', *Oxford Journal of Archaeology*, 10(1) 1991, 61–74

I. M. Stead, *Iron Age Cemeteries in East Yorkshire*, English Heritage, London, 1991

I. M. Stead and V. Rigby, *Verulamium, the King Harry Lane Site*, English Heritage, London, 1989

I. M. Stead, J. B. Bourke, D. Brothwell, *Lindow Man, the Body in the Bog*, British Museum Publications, London 1986

R. C. Turner and R. G. Scaife, *Bog Bodies: New Discoveries and New Perspectives*, British Museum Press, London, 1995

ART AND ARTEFACTS

J. W. Brailsford, *Early Celtic Masterpieces from Britain*, British Museum Publications, London, 1975

R. Hobbs, *British Iron Age Coins in the British Museum*, British Museum Press, London, 1996

P. de Jersey, *Celtic coinage of Iron Age Britain*, Shire Publications, Princes Risborough, 1996

R. Megaw and V. Megaw, *Celtic Art*, Thames and Hudson, London and New York, 1989

I. M. Stead, *The Battersea Shield*, British Museum Publications, London, 1985

I. M. Stead, *Celtic Art*, British Museum Press, rev. edn, 1996

SETTLEMENT AND LANDSCAPE

R. Bewlay, *Prehistoric Settlements*, Batsford/English Heritage, London, 1994 (especially chapter 6)

J. Coles and S. Minnitt, *'Industrious and fairly civilized': the Glastonbury Lake Village*, Somerset Levels Project and Somerset County Council, 1995

B. Cunliffe, *Danebury*, Batsford/English Heritage, London, 1993

P. J. Reynolds, *Iron Age Farm; the Butser Experiment*, British Museum Publications, London, 1979

N. M. Sharples, *Maiden Castle*, Batsford/English Heritage, London, 1991

G. Wainwright, *Excavations at Gussage-All-Saints*, HMSO Archaeological Report Series 10, 1979

RELIGION

A. King and G. Soffe, 'The Iron Age and Roman temple on Hayling Island', in A. P. Fitzpatrick and E. L. Morris (eds), 1994

S. Piggott, *The Druids*, 2nd edn, Thames and Hudson, London and New York, 1968

ACKNOWLEDGEMENTS

AUTHORS' ACKNOWLEDGEMENTS

The authors are grateful to many colleagues who gave advice, information and illustrations or just listened patiently to our ideas. Thanks are due particularly to Roger Featherstone, Karen Hughes, Catherine Johns, Sandra Marshall, Ian Stead and Carolyn Jones.

ILLUSTRATIONS

All illustrations courtesy of the Trustees of the British Museum (photographs by the BM Photographic Service) except for the following:

frontispiece RCHME, © Crown copyright, SU 0340/154
back cover RCHME, © Crown copyright, SY 6688/133

1 Simon James
2 Based on Ruth and Vincent Megaw 1989, fig. 2
4 Durham University, Department of Archaeology
5 Drawing by Karen Hughes, BM, based on Collis 1984, fig. 2, and other sources
6 Karen Hughes, BM
7 Karen Hughes, BM
8 © Society of Antiquaries of London
9 Léon Morel, *La Champagne Souterraine, Album*, 1898 pl. 7
12 John A. Kemble, *Horae Ferales*, (eds R. G. Latham and A. W. Franks, 1868, pl. xv
13 RCHME, © Crown copyright, SY 6688/133
21 Karen Hughes, BM, based on Elizabeth Crowfoot in Stead, 1991, fig. 79
24 Karen Hughes, BM
25 Stephen Crummy, BM
31 Karen Hughes, BM
38 Karen Hughes, BM
39 Karen Hughes, BM
45 Stephen Crummy, BM
57 Watercolour by Alan Sorrell

58 Illustrated London News Picture Library, ILN 2 Dec 1911
59 Simon James
60 A. L. Pacitto
61 RCHME, © Crown copyright, SU 0395/22
62 Simon James
63 Simon James
64 Aerofilms of Borehamwood, AC245508
65 © The Danebury Trust
66 © The Danebury Trust
76 I. M. Stead
77 A. L. Pacitto
78 I. M. Stead
81 After Stead and Rigby 1989, fig. 182
82 After A. King and G. Soffe, 1994, fig. 33.2
85 Karen Hughes, BM
86 From O. G. S. Crawford and A. Keiller, *Wessex from the Air*, Oxford University Press, 1928, pl. 1. RCHME © Crown copyright, Crawford Collection, no 246.
90 Simon James
92 A. L. Pacitto
96 Plan kindly provided by Rosalind Niblett

INDEX